NEW ESSAYS ON
THE PORTRAIT OF A LADY

★ The American Novel ★

GENERAL EDITOR

Emory Elliott
University of California, Riverside

Other books in the series:

New Essays on
The Portrait of a Lady

Edited by
Joel Porte

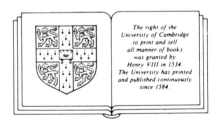

The right of the
University of Cambridge
to print and sell
all manner of books
was granted by
Henry VIII in 1534.
The University has printed
and published continuously
since 1584.

CAMBRIDGE UNIVERSITY PRESS

Cambridge

New York   Port Chester   Melbourne   Sydney

Published by the Press Syndicate of the University of Cambridge
The Pitt Building, Trumpington Street, Cambridge CB2 1RP
40 West 20th Street, New York, NY 10011, USA
10 Stamford Road, Oakleigh, Melbourne 3166, Australia

© Cambridge University Press 1990

First published 1990

Printed in the United States of America

Library of Congress Cataloging-in-Publication Data
New essays on The portrait of a lady / edited by Joel Porte.
p. cm. – (The American novel)
Includes bibliographical references (p.).
Contents: Introduction / Joel Porte – The portrait of a lady and
modern narrative / Donatella Izzo – The fatherless heroine and the
filial son / Alfred Habegger – The portrait of a lack / William
Veeder – Frail vessels and vast designs : a psychoanalytic portrait
of Isabel Archer / Beth Sharon Ash.
ISBN 0-521-34508-1. – ISBN 0-521-34753-X (pbk.)
1. James, Henry, 1843–1916. Portrait of a lady. I. Porte, Joel.
II. Series.
PS2116.P63N4   1990
813'.4 – dc20   89-27235

British Library Cataloguing in Publication applied for.

ISBN 0–521–34508–1 hard covers
ISBN 0–521–34753–X paperback

The portraits of William James in Chapter 4
are reproduced by permission of the Houghton
Library, Harvard University.

Contents

v

Contents

Series Editor's Preface

In literary criticism the last twenty-five years have been particularly fruitful. Since the rise of the New Criticism in the 1950s, which focused attention of critics and readers upon the text itself – apart from history, biography, and society – there has emerged a wide variety of critical methods which have brought to literary works a rich diversity of perspectives: social, historical, political, psychological, economic, ideological, and philosophical. While attention to the text itself, as taught by the New Critics, remains at the core of contemporary interpretation, the widely shared assumption that works of art generate many different kinds of interpretation has opened up possibilities for new readings and new meanings.

Before this critical revolution, many American novels had come to be taken for granted by earlier generations of readers as having an established set of recognized interpretations. There was a sense among many students that the canon was established and that the larger thematic and interpretative issues had been decided. The task of the new reader was to examine the ways in which elements such as structure, style, and imagery contributed to each novel's acknowledged purpose. But recent criticism has brought these old assumptions into question and has thereby generated a wide variety of original, and often quite surprising, interpretations of the classics, as well as of rediscovered novels such as Kate Chopin's *The Awakening*, which has only recently entered the canon of works that scholars and critics study and that teachers assign their students.

The aim of The American Novel Series is to provide students of American literature and culture with introductory critical guides to

American novels now widely read and studied. Each volume is devoted to a single novel and begins with an introduction by the volume editor, a distinguished authority on the text. The introduction presents details of the novel's composition, publication history, and contemporary reception, as well as a survey of the major critical trends and readings from first publication to the present. This overview is followed by four or five original essays, specifically commissioned from senior scholars of established reputation and from outstanding younger critics. Each essay presents a distinct point of view, and together they constitute a forum of interpretative methods and of the best contemporary ideas on each text.

It is our hope that these volumes will convey the vitality of current critical work in American literature, generate new insights and excitement for students of the American novel, and inspire new respect for and new perspectives upon these major literary texts.

Emory Elliott
University of California, Riverside

A Note on the Text

Because the 1881 and 1908 (New York Edition) versions of *The Portrait of a Lady* represent two quite distinct texts, and have been so treated in the critical literature, contributors to this volume have chosen to work with the one or the other depending on their own arguments and interests. In each case the text used is identified at the start of the essay, and subsequent references are by chapter. Citations from the original book publication of *Portrait* (1881) are drawn from the only conveniently available reprint, that edited by Oscar Cargill for the New American Library (Signet Classics) in 1963. Citations from the New York Edition text (1908) may most conveniently be found in the Norton Critical Edition, edited by Robert D. Bamberg (New York, 1975).

Introduction:
The Portrait of a Lady and "Felt Life"

JOEL PORTE

1

AMONG those novels of the nineteenth century which continue to be read and discussed as models of fictive craft and as major contributions to humanity's comprehension of itself, *The Portrait of a Lady* stands out for the complexity of its chief character, the compelling nature of its story, the density of its range of cultural reference, and the artfulness of its conception and execution. Like *Pride and Prejudice, Madame Bovary, Anna Karenina,* and *Middlemarch,* it focuses on the question of a woman's destiny and the conditions and consequences of modern marriage. But, like *The Scarlet Letter, Miss Ravenel's Conversion, A Modern Instance,* and *The Awakening,* it places those pressing issues in a specifically – indeed, uniquely – American context, in that international context of Americans returning to the Old World which was largely to define the work of Henry James.

Why was the "international theme" so central to James's work in general, and to *Portrait* in particular? For one thing, James considered it a "complex fate" to be an American, by which he meant, to take his phrase literally, that that fate was woven of many strands – European descent (for good or ill, James's world is resolutely Eurocentric), a Puritan background set against a developing libertarian tradition, a kind of self-imposed cultural barrenness, a presumptive innocence or at least detachment from the ills and iniquities of Europe, a sense of oneself as open to new opportunities and modes of self-definition. The list could go on, but a tentative point needs to be made: as distinct from the "provincial" works listed above, James's novels place most of his protagonists in a setting in which putative national characteristics are progressively tested and modified under the pressures of apparently alien circumstances. It is as if James wished, by way of experiment, to detach the individual strands of that "complex fate" and examine each cultural gene for its nature and influence. Europe was in effect the laboratory setting for his experiment – the matrix out of which these new creatures called Americans had evolved and to which, as to an abandoned and perhaps unrecognized parent, they needed to return for praise, punishment, advice, education, consolation, refreshment, reassurance, and ultimately a sense of their own identity. For to be an American is precisely to be defined by an "other," by something that has been left behind in the excitement of making oneself over. The return to origins represents the recapturing of a repressed past, the relearning of a language that one did not know one understood. For James, America was Europe in translation; his work amounts to a continual comparing of the two texts.

That work begins in some of the earliest tales and provides the themes for most of the major fiction of James's first period: *Roderick Hudson, Daisy Miller, The American, The Europeans,* and *The Portrait of a Lady.* What distinguishes *Portrait* is that the broad strokes of melodrama and conventional characterization – the hallmarks of James's apprenticeship – have been subtilized and subordinated for the sake of one thing: the portrait of an extraordinary young American woman "affronting her destiny." *Affronting,* not *confronting:* James's word appears to stress Isabel Archer's defiance, her boldness, her desire to put the world to the test. This, we might say, is the principal mark of Isabel's Emersonian spirit.[1] She seems to say, with the early Emerson, "You think me the child of my circumstances: I make my circumstance. . . . I – this thought which is called I, – is the mould into which the world is poured like melted wax. The mould is invisible, but the world betrays the shape of the mould. You call it the power of circumstance, but it is the power of me."[2] Who can resist this self-reliant representative of imperious American femininity? Those who surround her immediately enter her orbit. She winds a noble English lord around her finger; a strong-minded American businessman whose name is synonymous with the very latest method of spinning cotton is spun in emotional circles by this willful girl; a wealthy expatriate American banker is persuaded to leave her a fortune. How can one fail to admire the power of such virgin excellence and self-possession? No one can, apparently — least of all the sympathetic reader, who cheers Isabel on in her pride and refusal to be dissuaded from her own stern claims and perfect circle. Even Gilbert Osmond, who might strike some as a mere fortune-hunter, knows and appreciates the true American article when he sees it. Would he ever propose to a *merely* flirtatious and rattle-brained American princess like Daisy Miller? It will be a test of his *own* mettle and self-possession to harness so much innocently arrogant energy and turn it to his use.

Isabel, of course, like the elder Emerson of "Fate," will discover that "we have two things, — the circumstance, and the life. Once we thought, positive power was all. Now we learn, that negative power, or circumstance, is half."[3] That is both sobering and consoling, for it is not simply that life is swallowed up in circumstance but rather that it is qualified by it, reduced by half but not annihilated. Osmond represents "negative power," the force of the alien "other" that seems to be "European"; but, as we know, he too is an American — though one who has consented to worship at the altar of convention, propriety, whatever seems to be "aristocratic" and nonvulgar. Such "Osmondism" is also part of the American scene, though Isabel had been protected from it, perhaps by her romantic and free-spirited father. So, we might say, she had to travel to Europe to discover a type of specious aristocrat she could easily have met in America. But James has other fish to fry, for Europe will provide not only the trap for her innocence but also the opportunity for her to repossess her dignity and sense of freedom by identifying with those who have been compromised before her. Eventually Isabel will learn to take "old Rome into her confidence" (New York Edition, Chap. 49), and the city will repay that trust by taking her into *its* confidence, returning a measure of what she has lost. Thus, Isabel will learn the further Emersonian lesson of compensation — that things go by halves indeed, and that nothing can be considered purely evil. It is a question of reciprocity — "Europe" taming her "American" half, "America" finding a way to recoup its "European" loss by means that Europe itself provides. Why does Isabel need to leave Rome when it will contrive finally to meet her halfway?

Such a traditional humanistic reading of *Portrait*, whereby "America" and "Europe" stand as the metonymic poles of "innocence" and "experience" between which this essentially noble New World everywoman must negotiate her perilous way — a view reinforced by obvious Miltonic echoes in the book suggesting an archetypal "fall" from grace and expulsion from the "garden" at the hands of an egoistic "devil," leading to entry into an uncertain world of "choice" and the exercise of right reason[4] — such a familiar reading of *Portrait*, while clearly justified, is probably also inadequate. There is still something left over that baffles interpretation. So, for example, although the publication of *Portrait* in 1881 was greeted by a barrage of praise from leading critics — William Dean Howells in *The Century*, W. C. Brownell in *The Nation*, Horace Scudder in *The Atlantic Monthly*, John Hay in *The Tribune* — a persistent negative report also began to be heard. R. H. Hutton, writing in the *Spectator*, remarked of Isabel that "the reader never sees her, or realises what she is, from the beginning of the book to the close. She is the one lady of whom no portrait is given . . . the central figure remains shrouded in mist."[5] Margaret Oliphant, in *Blackwood's*, agreed, complaining that the book's title was unjustified, for "of the heroine, upon whom the greatest pains have been expended, and to whom endless space is afforded for the setting forth of her characteristics, we have no portrait."[6] So, too, *The Atheneum*: "There are, indeed, portraits of ladies enough and clear enough; the only one who is not portrayed so as to make the reader understand her is the heroine."[7] Even James's friend John Hay, turning this supposed defect into a virtue, noted that "the interest of the novel comes in great part from the vagueness of our acquaintance with Miss Archer."[8] And later critics amplified the point. Carl Van Doren, in 1921, spoke of the "never quite penetrable fiber of the heroine."[9] Quentin Anderson, in 1957, observed astutely that "the clarity, the light and sure touch, of the prose playing about the figure of Isabel only to reveal an obscurity, a

4

darkness within her lovely presence, has an effect which is among James's greatest achievements."[10]

Chiaroscuro — that is surely a principal Jamesian technique, refined from the work of Hawthorne. Isabel is presented initially as a creature of the sunshine whose perception is "clear" (Chap. 2) and who believes that one "should move in a realm of light" and of "happy impulse" (Chap. 6). But she is not, after all, the fair Rowena of Scottian romance; her eyes are grey, not blue, and her hair is "dark, even to blackness" (Chap. 5). Isabel figures her own nature as "garden-like" and therefore thinks of "introspection . . . [as] an exercise in the open air," but she is often reminded of other places, "dusky, pestiferous tracts, planted thick with ugliness and misery" (Chap. 6). She believes that "if a certain light should dawn she could give herself completely," but the image itself frightens her. This fine American girl, so hopeful-seeming and expansive, determined to "regard the world as a place of brightness" (Chap. 6), nevertheless finds herself attracted to the equivocal "golden air" of Gilbert Osmond's "early autumn" (Chap. 29). Her imagination goes forward to meet this obscure figure; yet, even as he declares himself, it hangs back, sensing that "there was a last vague space it couldn't cross — a dusky, uncertain tract which looked ambiguous and even slightly treacherous." At this point the author admits that his "young lady's spirit was strange," and informs us that she was to cross that tract despite its perilousness (Chap. 29). Isabel Archer — perversely, as it would seem — turns away from the light (as she will do on the last page of the novel) and walks steadily into the dusk.[11]

That last word represents James's figure for what appears to be Isabel's true destiny and desire throughout *Portrait*. Before she consents to marry Osmond, when the "world lay before her" and "she could do whatever she chose," Isabel chooses to walk alone through London in the "early dusk of a November afternoon" and positively enjoys the "dangers," losing "her way almost on purpose, in order to get more sensations" (Chap. 31). That quasi-Gothic indulgence in the pleasures of terror all too innocently prefigures a later scene, in which Isabel returns to London to be with the dying Ralph and feels helpless and anxious. Now she is glad that Henrietta is there to accompany her, for "the dusky, smoky, far-arching vault of the station, the strange, livid light, the dense, dark, pushing crowd" fills her with "nervous fear"; and she remembers how she enjoyed walking away from Euston station alone "in the winter dusk . . . five years before. She could not have done that to-day, and the incident came before her as the deed of another person" (Chap. 53).

Yes, we note, Isabel has changed, for she has taken the full measure of Osmond's shadowy world where the lights have been put out "deliberately, almost malignantly," and the "dusk [which] at first was vague and thin" has deepened and become "impenetrably black" (Chap. 42). But is she entirely different? Will James really permit us to believe that Isabel's taste for the *crépuscule* had nothing to do with her decision to marry Osmond? In Chapter 42 the author allows his heroine to be "very sure" that the shadows of Osmond's stifling spirit "were not an emanation from her own mind," but the reader may be excused for wondering. There *is* something obscure in the soul of this American woman – though we are assured she was not "a daughter of the Puritans" – that draws her to the dark tracts of experience.[12] Why, otherwise, at the end of the novel, when Caspar Goodwood glares at Isabel "through the dusk" and bestows the "white lightning" of his kiss, does she turn away in terror and feel that when the "darkness returned she was free"? That "certain light" to which, it is suggested in Chapter 6, Isabel "could give herself completely" has now apparently dawned but indeed proves "too formidable to be attractive" (Chap. 6).

If the "straight path" that Isabel discerns after turning away from Caspar and toward the darkness is viewed in Dantean terms, it gives a strangely ironic twist to the opening of the *Inferno*. There the poet finds himself in obscurity ("una selva oscura"), where the "straight path" is unclear ("che la diritta via era smarrita"), and eventually spends a long time working his way up to the light of paradise. But Isabel's "straight path" will apparently lead her back to Gilbert Osmond's hell and the obscurity of her own dusky nature. Just fourteen years after the appearance of *Portrait*, Thomas Hardy would produce a final novel dedicated to exploring the treacherous byways of modern sexuality and marriage, with a self-defeating "obscure" hero and a self-lacerating heroine who, like Isabel, marries a dessicated older man in the confusion of her own conflicted being. To deal with such painful cases, criticism would need to reach for a new vocabulary – and terms such as "neurotic"[13] – in place of James's more reticent notion of a protagonist whose character and fate could sufficiently be described as "complex."

2

The Portrait of a Lady first appeared in fourteen installments almost simultaneously in England (*Macmillan's Magazine,* October 1880 through November 1881) and America (*The Atlantic Monthly,* November 1880 through December 1881), exposing this first version of *Portrait* to a wide audience. Slightly revised, it was published in book form in both countries in November 1881. James's fees for the serial publication were considerable (more than $5,000), and his position in the magazine market was strengthened.[14] While *Portrait* could hardly be described as a best-seller, it was, according to George Monteiro, James's "largest commercial success" and became the object of much critical attention and comment.[15] Henceforth James would be known as the author of *The Portrait of a Lady.*

When the book reappeared in 1908 as part of the so-called New York Edition it had been subjected to James's own intense critical scrutiny and extensively revised. James thus established new terms for all future serious discussion of his one undisputed masterpiece: the two versions – of 1881 and of 1908 – would need to be compared as distinct though closely related literary-cultural artifacts. The work of comparing the two versions of *Portrait* has gone on for some time,[16] but the task has been rendered relatively simple for students since the appearance of the Norton Critical Edition of *Portrait* in 1975 with its textual appendix. What remains not simple at all is the question of how James's extensive rewriting of his earlier text affects the shape and meaning of the book.

One point of agreement among those who have studied James's revisions concerns precisely the erotic/neurotic element in the por-

7

trayal of Isabel. Almost a half-century ago, in the first and probably still the best serious study of James's revisions, F. O. Matthiessen observed that the 1908 text, especially in its rewritten conclusion, sharpens James's analysis of the "mixed repulsion and attraction"[17] in Isabel's reaction to Caspar Goodwood. His masculine hardness and aggressive quality are everywhere strengthened. And when Caspar returns at the end of the novel to carry Isabel away, her anxious awareness that "she had never been loved before," which in the first edition "wrapped her about" and "lifted her off her feet" — and it is important to notice that in this first version Isabel romantically figures her own sense of missed erotic opportunity as itself a lover who will embrace her and transport her somewhere — is considerably complicated:

> . . . she had never been loved before. She had believed it; but this was different; this was the hot wind of the desert, at the approach of which the others dropped dead, like mere sweet airs of the garden. It wrapped her about; it lifted her off her feet, while the very taste of it, as of something potent, acrid, and strange, forced open her set teeth. (Chap. 55)

We observe that with the addition of the desert figure the antecedent of *it*, in "it wrapped her about," has changed dramatically. Now it stands for the "hot wind" of sexual desire, which annihilates the sentimental-romantic and forces Isabel to taste something "potent, acrid, and strange" that, shockingly, suggests male seminal fluid.[18] As Matthiessen remarks, this "image takes [Isabel] as far away from her surroundings and the gentlemanly devotion of a Warburton as it does from the decadent egotism of an Osmond."[19]

In the face of such rewriting, I find it hard to agree with Anthony J. Mazzella that the later Isabel fears "a loss through the erotic of . . . the freedom of the mind to function unimpeded." She exists, he goes on, "supremely on the level of pure mind, and the erotic would destroy that existence."[20] Such a formulation confuses what we may infer to be Isabel's rationalizations with James's own purposes. Those purposes include the portrait of a woman deeply troubled — ambivalently attracted/repelled, fascinated/disgusted — by the conditions of physical love, who retreats to "mind" as a convenient nineteenth-century refuge from what James in 1908 seems to view as a distinctively twentieth-century (i.e., "modern") problem. It is surely significant that the Countess Gemini, in her revised revelation of the sordid background to the Osmond–Merle relationship, is made to react to Isabel's incomprehension by breaking out, "you've such a beastly pure mind. I never saw a woman with such a pure mind!" (Chap. 51). One can hardly believe that James intends the reader to sympathize entirely with a "pure mind" that remains so resistantly impervious to the truth. That oxymoronic "beastly pure" of the 1908 version pushes us toward the awareness that the "purity" of Isabel's mind, as a defense against and refuge from knowledge of the erotic, is itself suspect – a kind of "purity" within which lurks the very thing it fears.

Considering the evidence, it is equally difficult to accept Nina Baym's argument that the "rich mental life" James emphasizes in 1908 "effaces the original main quality of [Isabel's] character, emotional responsiveness," and that in 1908 "she is not a character likely to get swept away on a wave of feeling."[21] On the contrary, the Isabel of 1908 retains all of the responsiveness of 1881, with the addition of an even stronger reaction to erotic feeling. All of the "tears and anguish" (Chap. 54) characteristic of Isabel in the operatic deathbed scene with Ralph, for example, are retained. And her emotional response to Caspar Goodwood at the conclusion of the novel, as we have noticed, is if anything expanded. Not a sob or a tear is excised; Isabel's head in 1908 is described as "swimming"; and she replies to Caspar not by *saying* she wants him to leave but rather by *panting*. One can only agree with Matthiessen that James's revisions, in the main, the occasional "rococo flourish" notwithstanding, produce a "deepening of emotional tones."[22] Despite myriad changes in the texture of the novel – and it is by no means easy to see at each point what exactly James had in mind as he rewrote *Portrait* – the essential shape of the narrative, and of Isabel's character, remains intact. As I shall argue shortly, James's emphasis on "felt life" as the central criterion of value for author and protagonist alike remains sharply in focus.

James's Preface to *The Portrait of a Lady*, written a quarter of a century after the initial composition of the book, provides a vital link between the early and late versions of *Portrait*, drawing our attention to the central issues that had compelled James's imagination from the start and that continued to give form to the novel in its final version. The argument that James's Preface betrays his earlier intentions by forging a rationale for the 1908 version of the novel (i.e., by focusing on Isabel's "consciousness" as opposed to the emotional intensity and high romantic illusions of 1881)[23] overlooks the simple fact that James was not only engaged in describing his revisions but also in reviewing what he had done in the first place. The Preface, that is, represents for James both an astute rereading of the earlier text *and* an attempt to bring his sense of his subject up to date. But in some crucial particulars the Preface offers "nutritive and suggestive truth[s]" applicable to both versions.

One such makes its appearance right at the start of the Preface and disarmingly draws our attention to a large question in the Jamesian canon – the question of Italy. James recalls that he worked away at the book "during a stay of several weeks made in Venice" in 1880:

> . . . the waterside life, the wondrous lagoon spread before me, the ceaseless human chatter of Venice came in at my windows, to which I seem to myself to have been constantly driven, in the fruitless fidget of composition, as if to see whether, out in the blue channel, the ship of some right suggestion, of some better phrase, of the next happy twist of my subject, the next true touch for my canvas, mightn't come into sight.

Alas, James goes on, he searched in vain for his "next true touch," admonishing himself "that romantic and historic sites, such as the land of Italy abounds in, offer the artist a questionable aid to concentration when they themselves are not to be the subject of it. They are too rich in their own life and too charged with their own meanings merely to help him out with a lame phrase; they draw him away from his small question to their own greater ones."

James concludes these "rueful . . . reminiscences" by conceding that "one's book, and one's 'literary effort' at large," were undoubtedly improved by the Italian ambiance, for even a "wasted effort of attention" may prove "strangely fertilising." Though James does not attempt to speculate further about the significance of his Italian sojourn for the composition of *Portrait*, we at least may notice a curious echo, in his description of how Italy's "romantic and historic sites" draw the artist "away from his small question to their own greater ones," of a key scene late in the book: Isabel, in Chapter 49, takes a ride alone in "old Rome" and is compelled by the city's ruins to consider the "smallness" of her own sadness in the "large Roman record, and her haunting sense of the continuity of the human lot easily carried her from the less to the greater." A provisional conclusion might be that James, without entirely being aware of it, *was* strangely fertilized by the Italian scene as he framed his portrait of Isabel Archer – somehow carried from the lesser to the greater even as his heroine was to be.

That process – of being nourished by the Italian scene – was of course central to James's imagination throughout his career, and much critical attention has understandably been lavished on it.[24] It should suffice here, before we go on to explore more fully the question of Italy in *Portrait*, to dwell briefly on a few other examples, early and late. In the story, "Travelling Companions" (1870), a lovesick young man – whose name (Mr. Brooke) and marked sensibility are oddly proleptic of *Middlemarch*[25] – anticipates Isabel's lonely rides on the Roman Campagna when he betakes himself on horseback to the same place and somewhat too romantically meditates on "the tragical beauty of the scene." But Mr. Brooke, who is essentially in search of the picturesque and not the tragic, has a decidedly ambivalent response to the "sunny solitude and haunted vacancy" of the Campagna, experiencing a "mingled sense of exaltation and dread." The "potent sweetness and . . . high historic charm" give way to an air "so heavy with the exhalation of unburied death, so bright with sheeted ghosts," that this genial passionate pilgrim gallops back to the city and a rendezvous with his beloved. Though Mr. Brooke is far more alive than Daisy Miller would be to Rome's "deep interfusion" of "freshness" and "antiquity," its ominously double appeal – both to romantic expansiveness and to the imagination of danger and disaster – he is not a candidate for tragic awareness. Unlike Isabel Archer, whose "haunting sense of the continuity of the human lot" will console her for a wretched marriage, Mr. Brooke is on his way, presumably, to connubial bliss, and has no need of the Roman ghosts. Nor, obviously, is he prepared, like Lambert Strether of *The Ambassadors,* to savor the "medal-like Italian face" of the Roman artist Gloriani, with its "deep human expertness" and evidence of "terrible life behind it" (later echoed by another subtle Roman, Prince Amerigo in *The Golden Bowl,* who insists that "everything's terrible . . . in the heart of man"). James's belief in the capacity of Italy to nurture a sense of the dear old sacred terror of life is evident early and late in his work, and it is precisely this belief that informs Isabel Archer's deepening consciousness and her decision to return to Rome.

The *topos* of Italy as the site of the artist's most intense growth in self-culture had, of course – long before James started composing *Portrait* – entered the awareness of European and American writers with whose work James was clearly familiar (Goethe, Madame De Stael, Stendhal, Hawthorne). In particular, James's early reading of Walter Pater's *The Renaissance* (1873), with its moving penultimate chapter on the celebrated eighteenth-century German art critic Johann Joachim Winckelmann, undoubtedly sharpened his interest in that "ardent attraction towards the South" (Pater quoting Mme. De Stael) which would become the staple of so much of James's fiction.[26] Pater's Latin epigraph to the Winckelmann chapter – "et ego in Arcadia fui" – called attention to the mingling of desire and danger that would constitute the ambiguous lure of the dream of Italy in the imagination not only of James, but also of later writers from Thomas Mann to Tennessee Williams.[27] But James, as we have noted, was probably already familiar with Madame De Stael's *Corinne; ou l'Italie,* a popular novel published in 1807 that largely set the terms for nineteenth-century treatments of the theme.[28] Mme. De Stael's eponymous heroine, offspring of an Italian mother and a Scottish lord named Edgarmond, is an intense, raven-haired, sensuous *improvisatrice* who embodies the antinomies of light and dark that constitute the essence of the Romantic artist's interior struggle. ("You know me not," she tells her English suitor Oswald, Lord Nevil; "Of all my faculties, the most powerful is that of suffering. I was formed for happiness; my nature is confiding and animated; but sorrow excites me to a degree that threatens my reason, nay, my life. Be careful of me! My gay versatility serves me but in appearance: within my soul is an abyss of despair.")[29] The explicit metonym for Corinne's divided and ambiguous soul is Rome, a city whose nature, Mme. de Stael's heroine explains, "gives birth to reveries elsewhere unknown. She is as intimate with the heart of man as if the Creator made her the interpretess between his creatures and himself."[30] Rome, then, is presented quintessentially as the scene of self-investigation − an incitement to examination of the secrets of the human heart, with its complex yearning for both love and death.

Individual readers may decide for themselves to what extent Mme. De Stael's novel stimulated James's own imagination as he plotted his "Italian" fictions; but one direct link to *Portrait* is worth considering: we are told twice in the novel (Chaps. 26, 35) that Gilbert Osmond's mother was known as the "American Corinne" − a "distinguished" woman with "pretensions to elegant learning" who "published descriptive poems and corresponded on Italian subjects with the English weekly journals." James's original impulse in insinuating this detail into his text was unquestionably satiric and even slightly ludicrous, since everybody (at least in Transcendental circles) knew that the "American Corinne" was Margaret Fuller. James is suggesting, in effect, a rewriting of history whereby Fuller does not die in a wreck off Fire Island in 1850 returning *from* Italy but rather transports her children *to* Italy after the death of her husband and brings them up in an atmosphere of debased Romanticism that mocks the spiritual intensities of Mme. De Stael's *Corinne,* turning her beloved Italy into a commercial literary opportunity. Indeed, one telling detail is worth noting. In the earlier version of *Portrait* (Chap. 26) James described his "American Corinne" as having had "pretensions to 'culture.' " Undoubtedly he later considered this satire to be rather heavy-handed, for not only is Osmond *mère* simply disposed of, by the inverted commas, as an inane camp follower of the arts (thus belying the later description of her as "distinguished"); the arts and learning themselves seem hollowed out by the satiric emphasis implied in the concept of "culture."

James knew that this concept was a crucial one in his time and place; his earlier short-circuiting of the reader's response to the term would hardly do for the enriching artistic eye that he brought to his text twenty-five years later. Perhaps during 1880–81 James was secretly mocking his own callow response to Americans in Italy, as when he wrote to his mother from Florence in 1869 complaining of American vulgarity and noting that his countrymen and women seemed to represent "the elements of modern man with *culture* left out. It's the absolute and incredible lack of *culture* that strikes you in common travelling Americans."[31] A decade later, plotting his first "big" novel, James probably realized that he himself had been thinking like the Osmonds — rejecting his fellow Americans out of hand on the basis of a potted and limited concept of "culture" that was insufficient for the complex tale he had in mind. Ultimately James would see that "culture" and related terms needed to be deployed in a more subtle fashion, for they implied a concept of high seriousness in the pursuit of self-development that had touched some of the most influential minds of the century, from Goethe and Emerson through Arnold, Ruskin, and Pater. "Culture," as Alwyn Berland has pointed out,[32] meant not simply traveling to Europe to make an obligatory obeisance before the great artifacts of the past but something more active and serious — "not so much an achieved condition as a state of becoming, of striving." Culture implied something "like a religious vocation"; and Berland cites a passage from Pater's *Marius the Epicurean* that equates the concept of "culture" with a desire to "be perfect" — to achieve a "complete education." One might also cite passages in Pater's "Winckelmann" in which the aim of culture is defined as attaining "not only as intense but as complete a life as possible." The "pure instinct of self-culture," Pater argues, is not so much a question of acquiring "the forms of culture . . . as to find in them its own strength. The demand of the intellect is to feel itself alive."[33]

We should be able to hear palpitating within such definitions the impulse that drives Isabel Archer, however deludedly, to Italy and into the arms of Gilbert Osmond. James needed to purge from the earlier edition of *Portrait* his satiric allusions to "culture" precisely because they foreclosed the central issue of his tale: the fine art of learning to discriminate as the heart of spiritual growth and vitality. If Isabel mistakes Osmond in his Italian setting for the true votary of high culture, that is owing to her inexperience, not to the inadequacy of either Italy or the concept of "culture." The image of Osmond walking on his terrace above the Val d'Arno seemed to speak to Isabel "of the kind of personal issue that touched her most nearly" – and it certainly did: of the issue of "choice between objects, subjects, contacts – what might she call them? – of a thin and those of a rich association." Osmond's Florentine image bespeaks "a care for beauty and perfection so natural and so cultivated together that the career appeared to stretch beneath it in the disposed vistas and with the ranges of steps and terraces and fountains of a formal Italian garden" (Chap. 26). When "cultivation" appears so "natural" – not something applied *ab extra* but rather the organic growth of a spirit nurtured on the best that the Old World has to offer – how can it be false? Osmond seems to be *rooted* in the gracious Italian soil. Why then should he be taken for a parasite? And if he had spoken of his "provincial side" – he, a man of such exquisite worldliness – "was it a harmless paradox, intended to puzzle her? or was it the last refinement of high culture?" Isabel inclines to the Arnoldian reading of Osmond, taking him as an example of "standards and touchstones other than the vulgar" (Chap. 24). And why not? Osmond is so perfect an imitation that only a connoisseur could be expected to tell the difference. As Isabel insists to Ralph, "Osmond's simply . . . a very cultivated and a very honest man" (Chap. 34). That ambiguous "cultivated," added in the later edition of *Portrait,* marks Isabel's problem: the inability to tell the factitious from the real. But that is why James has sent her to Europe – not, with her presumably

15

superior intellect, to mock her fellow Americans' pretensions to "culture," but to learn the true meaning of the concept.

Italy functions intensely as the site of Isabel's aesthetic and spiritual education – her education in "culture" – not mainly owing to its monuments and museums but rather because of what James was to call the "sense of the past." Writing of Hawthorne and James shortly after the latter's death in 1916, T. S. Eliot praised Hawthorne's "very acute historical sense" and argued that his interest in "the deeper psychology" – particularly noted by James in his book on Hawthorne – culminates in James's "sense of the past": "James has taken Hawthorne's ghost-sense and given it substance."[34] By "ghost-sense" Eliot partly means to deprecate Hawthorne's employment of "Walter Scott–Mysteries of Udolpho upholstery" – the trappings of Gothic romance that beguiled American writers from Brockden Brown through Poe, Hawthorne, and Melville. As has been observed by such critics as Martha Banta, Elsa Nettels, and William Veeder,[35] James in fact drew deeply on the Gothic tradition in framing his *Portrait* – transforming Mrs. Radcliffe's *Mysteries of Udolpho*, for example, with its putative ghosts and goblins, and atmosphere of pervasive terror, into a drama of consciousness. Instead of a fair-haired ingenue from the Valais (Emily St. Aubert), impeccably innocent and staunchly virginal, we have an Emersonian free spirit, with a troubled half-awareness of her own sexuality; in place of the wicked aunt (Mme. Cheron), we have two cognate figures – Mrs. Touchett, with her laconic incommunicativeness, who unwittingly delivers Isabel into the hands of her betrayers, and the urbane Mme. Merle, whose smooth deceit overwhelms Isabel's provincial inexperience; and finally, most terribly, in place of an egregiously sinister Italian (Montoni), with an all-too-obviously frightening castle in the Appennines, we have an expatriate American whose fine manners, formal gardens, and exquisite objets d'art seem to belie the proverbial wisdom (as paraphrased by Carl Maves) that "un Americano italianato è un diavolo incarnato."[36]

To be sure, James does allow the requisite "castle-spectre" that Isabel romantically demands upon arriving at Gardencourt; though when it appears at her bedside late in the novel, after Ralph Touchett's death, it does so not as a Gothic revenant but rather as the objective correlative of Isabel's growth in the capacity to suffer. Her development of a "ghost-sense," her descent into the "deeper psychology," comes to be measured by Isabel's ceasing to view herself as a person living freely and innocently in an unbounded eternal present and her increasing awareness of herself as a contingent creature with a history and a destiny – at once personal and part of a larger collectivity. Isabel's growing sense of herself *in time*, ineluctably bound to patterns of experience that replicate the tragic fate of humankind, is nourished most potently by the Italian scene, at once enchanting and appalling, where the darkest aspects of accumulated human experience are deceptively cloaked (as they are in Gilbert Osmond) in "style." As James himself writes of southern Italy:

> . . . the beauty and the poetry, at all events, were clear enough, and the extraordinary uplifted distinction; but where, in all this, it may be asked, was the element of "horror" that I have spoken of as sensible? – what obsession that was not charming could find a place in that splendid light, out of which the long summer squeezes every secret and shadow? I'm afraid I'm driven to plead that these evils were exactly in one's imagination, a predestined victim always of the cruel, the fatal historic sense. To make so much distinction, how much history had been needed! So that the whole air still throbbed and ached with it, as with an accumulation of ghosts . . . [37]

The terrors and horrors that eventually come to haunt Isabel so effectively are thus to be viewed as the necessary concomitants of a "fatal historic sense" that she has repressed. When she recovers it most comprehensively – we shall shortly look again at Isabel's experience on the Roman Campagna in Chapter 49 – the terror and the horror are incorporated into a larger perspective that we may call "cultural."

4

Responding, just a few years after publishing *Portrait*, to the English novelist Walter Besant, who had argued that the English tradition in fiction was essentially "moral," James wrote "The Art of Fiction," his most important general treatment of the subject before the great Prefaces to the New York Edition.[38] Anticipating, in fact, his Preface to *Portrait*, James argued for the necessary freedom of the artist with regard to both subject and treatment as part of the "search for form." Rejecting the notion that there are "moral" and "immoral" fictions, he insisted on a more comprehensive view: "the only classification of the novel that I can understand is into that which has life and that which has not." The characters and situations which have life, "which strike one as real," are essentially those "that touch and interest one most." Over and over again James stressed the "quality of the mind of the producer" as the controlling factor in art – and by "mind" he clearly intended *sensibility*. The artist must be capable of *feeling* life generally and completely, of being so thoroughly in *touch* with reality that we as readers will "feel that we are touching the truth" as we read.

James's insistence on "solidity of specification" as a way of providing contact with reality for artist and reader alike leads naturally to the more general theory of "tangibility" in the Preface to *Portrait*, where James argues eloquently that the only significant question to be asked about a work of fiction is "is it valid, in a word, is it genuine, is it sincere, the result of some direct impression or perception of life?" As he goes on famously to say, "felt life" is the only meaningful criterion for a work of art. Life must be palpably, tangibly present to the writer; it must make a "mark . . . on the intelligence." Finally, it is the "enveloping air of the artist's humanity," his being in literal contact with the feelings of others, "which gives the last touch to the worth of the work."

Classically inclined readers might be reminded of Horace's advice to the artist – "si vis me flere, dolendum est / primum ipsi tibi" (if you wish to make me weep, you must suffer first yourself)[39] – though I shall shortly attempt to justify a preference for Virgil. But the point is clear enough, and clearly applicable to Isabel: though she wants to see ghosts – indeed claims to be "not afraid" of them – she *is* "afraid of suffering" and naively thinks she can have the one without the other. "It's not absolutely necessary to suffer; we were not made for that," she insists to Ralph (Chap. 5). And further, in response to his urging that she wishes to "drain the cup of experience," Isabel replies: "No, I don't wish to touch the cup of experience. It's a poisoned drink! I only want to see for myself." Whereupon Ralph retorts: "You want to see, but not to feel" (Chap. 15). The argument is thus joined at James's own level. As the architect of her own developing portrait, Isabel is booked for a shallow career – voyeurism and dilettantism – unless she opens herself to feeling. (And so we see the appeal of Osmond, the priggish pseudo-aesthete, to this "pure and proud . . . cold and dry" young woman [Chap. 6]. We learn later, when he actually pops the question, that Isabel is terrified at the thought of spending the accumulated passion stored in her internal bank, for "if she touched it, it would all come out" [Chap. 29]. She would then, presumably, feel depleted, drained, *vulnerable* – in the literal sense of opening herself to being hurt.) Nothing Isabel can say or do or conceive, as the work of her ongoing portrait, will possibly interest us unless she learns the art of *tangibility* – of touching and being touched. But at this point she seems resolute in her desire to remain *intacta*.[40]

As some critics have already observed,[41] James threads through this novel, which – he confided to his notebooks – could "with strong handling . . . be very true, very powerful, very touching," a set of variations on his key term, beginning in Chapter 7:

> "My excuse for not rowing is that my cousin rows so well," said Ralph. "She does everything well. She touches nothing that she doesn't adorn!"
> "It makes one want to be touched, Miss Archer," Lord Warburton declared.
> "Be touched in the right sense and you'll never look the worse for it," said Isabel.

This bit of portentous paronomasia begins as elegant banter almost in the eighteenth-century manner (Ralph's epigram is reminiscent of Dr. Johnson's epitaph for Oliver Goldsmith),[42] takes an earnest emotional and perhaps sexual turn in Lord Warburton's response, and ends in a sort of conundrum with Isabel's puzzling advice. In any case the conscious overdetermination with which James deploys this rich term makes it difficult to delimit what he sets in play. To a reader who has already been through the book, multiple ironies are evident. Isabel will shortly acquire the golden "touch" and adorn the career and bank balance of Gilbert Osmond. But of course Warburton neither needs nor wants to be touched in this fashion. As a beautiful woman, Isabel would naturally be a singular adornment to Warburton's life, and he hopes that she will "touch," or come to him, in that way. He would also naturally want to be "touched," or tried, so that he might prove his value. But to be "touched" additionally means to be "afflicted," and Warburton is clearly already far gone in love-sickness. Isabel's sexual touch — like the traditional king's or queen's touch — would cure him of that scrofula, or swelling. For Isabel, however, being "touched" with love-madness is a distortion of the human. She wants to be admired but not "touched" sexually — that is, presumably, spotted or marked by desire, the active need for another person. Still, what Isabel means by "the right sense" is not at all clear. Indeed, that is precisely what she will need to learn. Among other things she will discover, horribly, that Osmond's putting the "touch" on her for her money without truly loving her, without wanting to touch or be touched affectively and sexually, is a last refinement of cruelty that will leave her "strangely married" (Chap. 42). Like his sometime consort Mme. Merle, who "touched the piano with a discretion of her own" — namely, *"du bout des doigts"* (Chap. 18) — Osmond too keeps the vulgar world at a distance. But when he does condescend to meddle, as Isabel learns to her cost, it is only to display "his faculty for making everything wither that he touched" (Chap. 42). Unlike the healing laying-on of hands attributed to authentic royalty, the touch of this "demoralised prince in exile" (Chap. 23) is a "blight" that demonstrates finally what it means to be touched in the wrong sense.

This much should be clear: James's belief that a truly moral fiction is not essentially an abstraction but rather the expression of an empathetic relation to the world in the concrete fullness of its being finds its direct parallel in Isabel's aesthetic education — that is, in her learning, to cite Dorothy Van Ghent, that "aesthetic experience proper, since it is acquired through the senses, is an experience of *feeling*. But so also moral experience, when it is not sheerly nominal and ritualistic, is an experience of *feeling*. Neither one has reality – has psychological depth – unless it is 'felt.' "[43] Isabel's growth as the artist of her own "felt life" amounts to a crash course in the Arnoldian/Paterian theory of self-culture. She must first learn to be objectively critical – "to see the object as in itself it really is," as Pater observes, quoting Arnold. Then she will be in a position to move on to "aesthetic criticism" – namely, to knowing "one's own impression as it really is." Our education, Pater continues, "becomes complete in proportion as our susceptibility to . . . impressions increases in depth and variety."[44] Hence Pater goes on to praise "the native tendency of Winckelmann to escape from abstract theory to intuition, to the exercise of sight and touch." Winckelmann came to apprehend the subtleties of classical art "not through the understanding, but by instinct or touch." Like Columbus discovering a new world, he developed "new senses fitted to deal with it. He is in touch with it . . . "[45] Isabel, too, in her strange voyage back to the heart of the Old World, must develop new senses in order to put herself "in touch with it."

That last phrase, finally, must be our "touchstone," in the Arnoldian sense, for an adequate reading of *Portrait* in its cultural setting. Being "in touch" with the accumulated experience of humankind, for Isabel – as for so many of James's most impressive heroines and heroes – involves sounding the depths of human distress and developing adequate strategies for dealing with such knowledge. James's brother William, in his *Varieties of Religious Experience*, would essentially define the "religious" sense as the recognition of the necessity for pity, sacrifice, acceptance, and renunciation in the face of life's tragedies and terrors. The "athletic attitude" – the resolute determination to exercise one's will (we may think of Caspar Goodwood) – simply cannot work, he argues, "when the organism begins to decay, or when morbid fears invade the mind." Then what we crave "is to be consoled in [our] very powerlessness, to feel that the spirit of the universe recognizes and secures [us], all decaying and failing as [we are]."[46]

This mood of melancholy awareness and stoic acceptance of pain and suffering – what we might call the "elegiac" mood – suffuses the second half of *Portrait,* as it does much of James's later work; and it was an equally notable characteristic of his literary generation, both in America and abroad, from Henry Adams through Pater and the so-called "decadents" of the 1880s and 1890s. Pater himself, for example, in a chapter of *Marius the Epicurean* entitled "Sunt Lachrimae Rerum," has his philosophical protagonist reflect that "we are constructed for suffering."[47] Since the days of Rome's legendary second king, Numa, there has come to be "a capacity for sorrow" in the human heart "which grows with all the growth, alike of the individual and of the race, in intellectual delicacy and power." There is, Marius continues, "a certain grief in things as they are, in man as he has come to be . . . some inexplicable shortcoming, or misadventure, on the part of nature itself," which he attributes to the ubiquity of death and all the small deaths that make up experience – "of remorse, of loss and parting, of outraged attachments." Even if men and women were perfect, he argues, and selfishness were banished, "there would still be this evil in the world, of a certain necessary sorrow and desolation." What is needed in the world to counteract this vein of evil "is a certain permanent and general power of compassion – humanity's standing force of self-pity – as an elementary ingredient in our social atmosphere, if we are to live at all." And as the emblem and touchstone of the sorrowful awareness that breeds healthful self-pity Pater cites Virgil's celebrated line from the first book of the *Aeneid,* from which he draws his chapter title – *Sunt lachrimae rerum et mentem mortalia tangunt* – and offers as a partial gloss, "Men's fortunes touch us!"

Here we have the key to Isabel's story. And the fact that Pater's *Marius* was published in 1885, four years after *Portrait,* is surely beside the point – or rather, it makes the point in cultural terms, suggesting how widespread Virgil's elegiac mood had become. Perhaps we are to assume that Isabel had conned her Virgil, for are we not told that she was "a prodigy of learning, a creature reported to have read the classic authors – in translations" (Chap. 6)? It is probable, at least, that her creator was no stranger to the familiar line in its original form, for he tells us that as a boy he "worried out Virgil" under the tutelage of a certain Monsieur Verchère and consequently "was almost conscious of the breath of culture as I modestly aspired to culture."[48] In any case, Isabel's most complete awareness of culture as a continuity of thought and emotion in which she finds her own strength occurs in this intensely Virgilian moment in Chapter 49 that marks the culmination of her Roman experience:

> Isabel took a drive alone that afternoon; she wished to be far away, under the sky, where she could descend from her carriage and tread upon the daisies. She had long before this taken old Rome into her confidence, for in a world of ruins the ruin of her happiness seemed a less unnatural catastrophe. She rested her weariness upon things that had crumbled for centuries and yet still were upright; she dropped her secret sadness into the silence of lonely places, where its very modern quality detached itself and grew objective, so that as she sat in a sun-warmed angle on a winter's day, or stood in a mouldy church to which no one came, she could almost smile at it, and think of its smallness. Small it was, in the large Roman record, and her haunting sense of the continuity of the human lot easily carried her from the less to the greater. She had become deeply, tenderly acquainted with Rome; it interfused and moderated her passion. But she had grown to think of it chiefly as the place where people had suffered. This was what came to her in the starved churches, where the marble columns, transferred from pagan ruins, seemed to offer her a companionship in endurance and the musty incense to be a compound of long-unanswered prayers. There was no gentler nor less consistent heretic than Isabel; the firmest of worshippers, gazing at dark altar-pictures or clustered candles, could not have felt more intimately the suggestiveness of these objects nor have been more liable at such moments to a spiritual visitation.

What is remarkable here, first, is the way in which the intensely personal nature of Isabel's suffering has been caught up into the larger human record. Emerson had argued years before, in "Self-Reliance," that a true devotee of "self-culture" would not need to travel to Italy "with the hope of finding somewhat greater than he knows."[49] But Isabel has discovered that the "greater" is precisely that which she did not know – that which lay beyond the narrow precincts of self-awareness. The traveler merely "carries ruins to ruins," Emerson had warned. But Isabel has found amid the ruins of Rome not simply the double of her own despair but rather a solace and consolation – a way of rendering the subjective objective, of seeing herself from the outside. It was romantic and foolish of her to think of the European experience as no more than the opportunity for a Gothic frisson – a private thrill at seeing crumbling castles and predictable ghosts. Now the "Gothic" has been filled with real substance, for Isabel has developed a "haunting sense of the continuity of the human lot." James's Hawthornian "ghost-sense" has been invested with new meaning, so that Isabel, as the connoisseur of art in its greater affective and historical setting, is susceptible to a true "spiritual visitation."

Carrying "her sombre spirit from one familiar shrine to the other," James tells us, Isabel finally "felt the touch of a vanished world" (Chap. 49). She has achieved the goal of the Jamesian artist, reaching out to gather the "felt life" of a world which is gone and subsuming her own suffering in it.[50] The enveloping air of what might now be called her own "artist's humanity" is in the process of giving the "last touch to the worth of the work." And so James concludes his magnificent passage in Chapter 49 by allowing Isabel to compose her best, most comprehensive portrait:

> The carriage, leaving the walls of Rome behind, rolled through narrow lanes where the wild honeysuckle had begun to tangle itself in the hedges, or waited for her in quiet places where the fields lay near, while she strolled further and further over the flower-freckled turf, or sat on a stone that had once had a use and gazed through the veil of her personal sadness at the splendid sadness of the scene – at the dense, warm light, the far gradations and soft confusions of colour, the motionless shepherds in lonely attitudes, the hills where the cloud-shadows had the lightness of a blush.

Is it fanciful to see in this fine long sentence the portrait which the book has promised? Not, we may note, like the other portraits in the novel, in which a charming young girl or gracious "lady" is self-consciously "framed" in a "gilded doorway" (Chap. 37), but rather a fully socialized portrait composed by Isabel herself as she sits "on a stone that had once had a use" – in a place that has been a part of human work — and matches her own sad countenance against the responsive "splendid sadness" of a scene that includes both nature and the human figure.[51] "I know that nothing else expresses me," Isabel had burst out long before, in her passionate Emersonian response to Mme. Merle's disquisition on "things" (Chap. 19). Now we see, without being told, the extent to which Isabel has come to be expressed by the full human scene which she has consented to be a part of.

We should remember, too, that Virgil's famous line is uttered by Aeneas, on his way to found Rome, as he stands before a wall painting in Carthage that depicts the fall of Troy — that is, his own recent history. The tears that he freely sheds as he muses on the tears that suffuse human experience are inspired by a picture. Mortal life touches the mind and heart most, we are led to understand, when it is mediated by art. And so Aeneas turns to his faithful friend Achates and counsels him to "put away fear," for — in some fashion or other — the telling of their story will bring salvation. Thus Aeneas spoke, reports the poet, and "nourished his soul" on what was after all little more than a painted portrait. We may be expected to do the same.

5

To judge by the level of critical interest it has sustained — hundreds of essays and at least six previous book-length collections — *The Portrait of a Lady* has been and continues to be a major source of nourishment for readers of James's fiction. If not James's most "popular" novel, it is arguably his most appealing — accessible yet rich in its literary texture, culturally resonant in its handling of the international theme, memorable both for the interest of its protagonist and her predicament and for its colorful supporting cast. Gilbert Osmond alone wins the prize as James's most magnificent villain; indeed, as a recent critic asserts, "there are few creepier beings in the history of literature."[52] How James managed to re-shape a more or less traditional and conventional tale of young innocence betrayed into such a psychologically and culturally compelling novel remains a wonder and to some extent a mystery

– hence the formidable volume of commentary. There is not likely to be a moratorium on studies of *Portrait*, especially at a time when the "woman question," as it was called in James's day, has come powerfully into focus both for its social relevance and for its value as an interpretive frame.

Three of the essays in this collection may be gathered within the ample categories of "feminist" or "gender" studies. Alfred Habegger's presentation of "deep background" for *Portrait* is based on wide reading in what Nina Baym has described as "women's fiction."[53] Habegger's analysis attempts to unravel some of the complexity of James's reaction to more conventional contemporary tales of female orphans who find themselves under the "protection" of older father-surrogate figures (as in his own *Watch and Ward*). Habegger offers us the most probing treatment we have had so far of James's relations with his cousin Minny Temple – the independent-minded woman who died of tuberculosis at age 24 and subsequently influenced the treatment both of Isabel Archer and of Milly Theale in *The Wings of the Dove* – especially as those relations impinge on James's complex reaction to his father's role as patriarch and commentator on women and marriage. William Veeder, in his "The Portrait of a Lack," boldly confronts the cognate question of James's own sexuality and sexual identity, speculating on how James's sense of "negativity" and his homoerotic bond to his brother William might be said to inform his elaboration of the Freudian "family romance" in *Portrait*. In the final essay devoted to feminist or gender issues, Beth Ash explores both the theoretical and textual implications of the missing mother in James's portrait of Isabel Archer. Drawing on recent revisions of Freudian ego-theory – especially among the French psychoanalytic community – Ash provides a considerably updated and sophisticated view of Isabel's "neurotic" temperament, especially as regards her repetition of sadomasochistic patterns deeply encoded in the repressed maternal imago that Ash views as the controlling element in Isabel's career.

The opening essay of the collection may be described as more "formalist" in its approach. Donatella Izzo's treatment of *Portrait* as "an autonomous linguistic object governed by its own laws" in the

European novelistic tradition established by Flaubert challenges a naively mimetic reading of James's novel in favor of an approach more centrally focused on James's contribution to the craft of narrative. Originally published in Italy as a chapter in a general introduction to James, Izzo's essay stands here also as a representative of the considerable interest that James has excited among European critics and writers, who tend to view his work less exclusively as a native American product.

Taken together these four essays provide a perspective on *The Portrait of a Lady* that is decidedly new, shifting attention from Isabel's moral or aesthetic education to those issues which may be said to undergird or control more traditional readings of the novel. Not, I must insist emphatically, that the more traditional readings (variations on which I have offered earlier) are wrong or outmoded. Rather, they are already sufficiently represented in the secondary literature. Readers of this collection may want to consider how these fresh interpretations reactivate some of the concerns of earlier critics of the novel, but in a different key. That transposition helps us to figure the work of interpretation as an ongoing symphony which does not repudiate its previous movements but rather develops them, from the same germ, into rich new forms. One hopes that Henry James himself would approve of this continuing process of critical revision and exfoliation, since he concludes his own Preface to *Portrait* by insisting that "there is really too much to say." We at least may take as paradigmatic Pablo Picasso's reply to a criticism of *his* portrait of Gertrude Stein: "everybody says that she does not look like it but that does not make any difference, she will."[54]

NOTES

1. This has been a staple of criticism for some time. See, for example, Philip Rahv, *Image and Idea* (Norfolk, Conn.: New Directions, 1949); Richard Chase, *The American Novel and Its Tradition* (New York: Anchor Books, 1957); Quentin Anderson, *The American Henry James* (New Brunswick, N.J.: Rutgers University Press, 1957); Richard

Poirier, *The Comic Sense of Henry James* (New York: Oxford University Press, 1960); and Paul John Eakin, *The New England Girl* (Athens: University of Georgia Press, 1976).

2. "The Transcendentalist," in *Essays and Lectures,* ed. Joel Porte (New York: Library of America, 1983), p. 196.

3. Ibid., p. 949.

4. Arnold Kettle calls *Portrait* "a nineteenth-century *Paradise Lost,*" in William T. Stafford, *Perspectives on James's Portrait of a Lady* (New York: New York University Press, 1967), p. 97. Cf. Robert Weisbuch, *Atlantic Double-Cross* (Chicago: University of Chicago Press, 1986), pp. 291–4.

5. In Alan Shelston, ed., *Washington Square and The Portrait of a Lady: A Casebook* (London: Macmillan, 1984), pp. 81–2.

6. Ibid., p. 89.

7. In Stafford, *Perspectives,* p. 40.

8. See George Monteiro, *Henry James and John Hay* (Providence: Brown University Press, 1965), p. 69.

9. In Shelston, *Casebook,* p. 109.

10. *American Henry James,* p. 198.

11. Cf. David Galloway, *Henry James: The Portrait of a Lady* (London: Edward Arnold, 1967), p. 31, and Charles Feidelson, "The Moment of *The Portrait of a Lady,*" in Robert D. Bamberg, ed., *The Portrait of a Lady,* Norton Critical Edition (New York: Norton, 1975), pp. 749–50. John Auchard, *Silence in Henry James: The Heritage of Symbolism and Decadence* (University Park: Pennsylvania State University Press, 1986), pp. 55–75, views Isabel under the rubric of the Baudelairean decadent who says "je cherche . . . le noir."

12. Juliet McMaster, "The Portrait of Isabel Archer," *American Literature* 45 (1973): 65, observes that "Isabel's own Puritan morality unites . . . with her psychological perversity."

13. See, for example, Albert J. Guerard, *Thomas Hardy* (Cambridge, Mass.: Harvard University Press, 1949), p. 109 and p. 170, note 144.

14. Useful information on James's literary income and analysis of his position in the literary marketplace may be found in Michael Anesko, *"Friction with the Market": Henry James and the Profession of Authorship* (New York: Oxford University Press, 1986).

15. See Monteiro, *Henry James and John Hay,* p. 155.

16. Major studies of James's revisions are F. O. Matthiessen, "The Painter's Sponge and the Varnish Bottle," in *Henry James: The Major Phase* (New York: Oxford University Press, 1944), pp. 152–86; Sidney J. Krause, "James's Revisions of the Style of *The Portrait of a Lady,*"

American Literature 30 (1958): 67–88; Anthony J. Mazzella, "The New Isabel," in Bamberg, Norton *Portrait,* pp. 597–619; Nina Baym, "Revision and Thematic Change in *The Portrait of a Lady,*" *Modern Fiction Studies* 22 (1976): 183–200 (reprinted in Shelston, *Casebook,* 184–202); and Lyall H. Powers, "Visions and Revisions: The Past Rewritten," in *Henry James Review* 7 (1986): 105–16. Hershel Parker offers a critical review of scholarly treatments of James's revisions in *Flawed Texts and Verbal Icons: Literary Authority in American Fiction* (Evanston, Ill.: Northwestern University Press, 1984), pp. 85–114.

17. Matthiessen, *Major Phase,* p. 178.
18. On Isabel's resistance to "penetration" see Dennis L. O'Conner, "Intimacy and Spectatorship in *The Portrait of a Lady,*" *Henry James Review* 2 (1980): 25, and Carren Kaston, *Imagination and Desire in the Novels of Henry James* (New Brunswick, N. J.: Rutgers University Press, 1984), p. 54. Kaston's argument that "James has given Caspar a sexual identity which justifies Isabel's fearful associations of eroticism with violence" overlooks the fact that throughout the novel – and especially here – we see Caspar emphatically as Isabel's imagination conceives him.
19. Matthiessen, *Major Phase,* p. 179.
20. In Bamberg, Norton *Portrait,* pp. 610–11.
21. In Shelston, *Casebook,* pp. 185, 188.
22. Matthiessen, *Major Phase,* pp. 160, 171.
23. See, for example, Baym in Shelston, *Casebook,* pp. 185–6.
24. See Robert L. Gale, "Henry James and Italy," in *Studi Americani* 3 (1957); Cristina Giorcelli, *Henry James e L'Italia* (Rome: Edizioni di Storia e Letteratura, 1968); and Carl Maves, *Sensuous Pessimism: Italy in the Work of Henry James* (Bloomington: Indiana University Press, 1973).
25. The name of Mr. Brooke's sweetheart – Miss Evans – strengthens the association with George Eliot, whose real name was Mary Ann Evans Cross.
26. Walter Pater, *The Renaissance* (London: Macmillan, 1900), p. 179. On James's interest in and attitude toward Pater see Adeline R. Tintner, "Pater in *The Portrait of a Lady* and *The Golden Bowl,* including Some Unpublished Henry James Letters," *Henry James Review* 3 (1982): 80–95, though I think that Tintner's treatment unduly overemphasizes the negative component in James's reaction to Pater. Similarly, Lynda S. Boren, in "Undoing the *Mona Lisa*: Henry James's Quarrel with da Vinci and Pater," *Mosaic* 20 (1987): 100, argues that "in the attitudes

and character of Gilbert Osmond, James attacks the esthetics of Pater's philosophy."

27. The form of Pater's Latin tag – "I too lived in Arcady" – seems, in typical nineteenth-century fashion, to stress the wistful and elegiac nature of Winckelmann's attachment to Italy, but Pater must have known that in its original form – "et in Arcadia ego" ("even in Arcady I, Death, hold sway") – it served as a memento mori in the midst of sensuous pleasure. See Erwin Panofsky, "*Et in Arcadia Ego*: Poussin and the Elegiac Tradition," in his *Meaning in the Visual Arts* (New York: Doubleday, 1955).

28. Lynda S. Boren, "Undoing the *Mona Lisa*," p. 98, touches briefly on James's interest in *Corinne*.

29. Madame De Stael, *Corinne; or, Italy,* trans. Isabel Hill (New York: Derby & Jackson, 1858), pp. 78–9.

30. Ibid., pp. 88–9.

31. *Letters of Henry James,* ed. Leon Edel (Cambridge, Mass.: Harvard University Press, 1972), vol. 1, p. 152: cited in Lyall H. Powers, "Visions and Revisions," p. 109.

32. See *Culture and Conduct in the Novels of Henry James* (Cambridge: Cambridge University Press, 1981), esp. pp. 1–37.

33. Pater, *The Renaissance,* pp. 188, 229.

34. T. S. Eliot, "Henry James: The Hawthorne Aspect," in Edmund Wilson, *The Shock of Recognition* (New York: Modern Library, 1943), pp. 858–65. Eliot's essay was originally published in the *Little Review* in 1918.

35. See Martha Banta, *Henry James and the Occult* (Bloomington: Indiana University Press, 1972); Elsa Nettels, "'The Portrait of a Lady' and the Gothic Romance," *South Atlantic Bulletin* 39 (1974): 73–82; William Veeder, *Henry James: The Lessons of the Master* (Chicago: University of Chicago Press, 1975).

36. *Sensuous Pessimism,* p. 70: "An italianate American is a devil incarnate."

37. *Italian Hours* (New York: Horizon Press, 1968), p. 493.

38. Reprinted in *The Art of Fiction and Other Essays,* ed. Morris Roberts (New York: Oxford University Press, 1948), pp. 3–23. "The Art of Fiction" was originally published in 1884.

39. *Epistles,* Book II, 3, lines 102–103.

40. Cf. Dennis L. O'Conner, "Intimacy and Spectatorship," p. 26.

41. See Galloway, *Henry James,* p. 26, note 1; Mary Jane King, "The Touch of the Earth: A Word and a Theme in *The Portrait of a Lady,*"

Nineteenth-Century Fiction 29 (1974): 345–7; and Robert White, "Love, Marriage, and Divorce: The Matter of Sexuality in *The Portrait of a Lady,"* *Henry James Review* 7 (1986): 63.

42. "He touched nothing that he did not adorn." In view of Dr. Johnson's obvious pun on Goldsmith's name we may notice how Ralph's presumably gallant remark proleptically hints at Isabel's coming into a fortune.

43. Dorothy Van Ghent, in Stafford, *Perspectives,* p. 120. It is worth noting that in the 1890s Bernard Berenson would develop and popularize a theory of "tactile values" in art appreciation that apparently owed something to William James if not to Henry. See Ernest Samuels, *Bernard Berenson: The Making of a Connoisseur* (Cambridge, Mass.: Harvard University Press, 1979), chapter 16, "The Tactile Imagination," esp. p. 229.

44. Pater, *The Renaissance,* pp. viii, ix.

45. Ibid., pp. 184, 193, 194.

46. *The Writings of William James,* ed. John J. McDermott (New York: Modern Library, 1968), pp. 754–5.

47. See *Marius the Epicurean* (London: Macmillan, 1900), chapter 25.

48. Henry James, *Autobiography,* ed. F. W. Dupee (New York: Criterion Books, 1956), p. 243.

49. *Essays and Lectures,* p. 278.

50. Cf. Dorothy Van Ghent, in Stafford, *Perspectives,* p. 120: "It is Rome *felt,* felt as an immensity of human time, as a great human continuum of sadness and loneliness and passion and aspiration and patience; and it has this definition by virtue of Isabel's personal ordeal and her perception of its meaning."

51. Cf. Giorcelli, *Henry James e L'Italia,* p. 47, who notes that Isabel here "establishes an authentic dialogue between her own sad spirit and the sadness of the place . . . we are in the realm of the *paysage moralisé,* of a scene that is at once real and a comprehensive representation of the character."

52. Weisbuch, *Transatlantic Double-Cross,* p. 284.

53. Nina Baym, *Women's Fiction* (Ithaca: Cornell University Press, 1978).

54. Gertrude Stein, *The Autobiography of Alice B. Toklas* (New York: Vintage Books, 1955), p. 12.

2

The Portrait of a Lady
and Modern Narrative

DONATELLA IZZO

Translated by Cristina Bacchilega

T HE publication of *Madame Bovary* in 1857 marks a turning point in narrative tradition. With Flaubert the novel, anticipating twentieth-century concerns, begins to reflect on itself: as Jean Rousset remarks, "it becomes critical and self-critical and it severs itself from the existing novel."[1]

Writers such as Sterne and Diderot had already displayed a profound awareness of form by violating literary conventions to expose their artifice; but in the eighteenth century, the novel was a fluid, not yet rigorously codified form, a fact which makes Flaubert's position quite different from Sterne's and Diderot's. To oversimplify the history of the novel's form and of the concept of mimesis, we might say that during the eighteenth century and the first half of the nineteenth century, by presenting itself as an imitation of life and a mirror of mores, the novel had codified its form and had recognized its physiognomy and theoretical justification in realism. It is commonplace to put Balzac at the climax of this tradition: *Eugénie Grandet* was published in 1833 and *l'Avant-propos* to the *Comédie Humaine* in 1842. Flaubert then works against the backdrop of this established conception of the novel, a well-defined and strong tradition, and disrupts it from within. In doing so, he self-consciously places himself in a new tradition of critical reflection on and within the novel — the common denominator of experiments otherwise as diverse as those of Proust,

My special thanks go to Professor Paola Cabibbo of "La Sapienza" University, Rome. Her friendship and generosity, as well as the insights she contributed during endless conversations about James, art, and criticism, helped me more than I can say.

Joyce, and Faulkner and which nowadays we see as the mark of twentieth-century art.

The text reclaims its self-referential nature – that is, its identity as an autonomous linguistic object governed by its own laws, rather than as a transparent vehicle between an external referent (the world, "reality") and the reader. In *Madame Bovary* we can detect this departure from the tradition of realism as much in the characters, story, and themes as in the organization of narrative discourse. Flaubert makes use of irony to devalue the concept of character as center of awareness and subject of experience; he devalues the story (*fabula* in Propp's terminology), those dramatic events which ought to reveal characters and themes, by arranging them in unconventional sequences; he devalues themes as moral statements and conclusions by systematically frustrating all attempts by his reader to draw a "message" from the novel. In other words, he radically questions the referential "content" of language and, thereby, its mimetic function. He creates a world which certainly appears to be real, but refuses to become meaningful, refuses to be interpreted on the basis of generic conventions, refuses to be recognized as a meaningful imitation of reality. By hindering the customary transactions of recognition that the reader negotiates with a text in order to draw meaning from it, Flaubert breaks the contract between writer and reader; moreover, behind the continuously sliding points of view from which events and characters are presented, it is finally impossible to detect a voice attributable to the author, a voice which will convey univocal messages and guarantee the reader a "correct" perspective.[2]

The Portrait of a Lady is revolutionary in ways which remind us of *Madame Bovary*, employing strategies which, though different from Flaubert's, point in the same direction: they affirm the self-referential nature, the autonomy, of the novel. The pairing of these two authors – who shared similar creative ideals and can now be recognized as precursors and masters of many twentieth-century novelistic techniques – as well as of their novels, is anything but arbitrary. In fact, *Madame Bovary* and *The Portrait of a Lady* display more than a thematic and technical affinity; indeed, James's novel – for all its perfect autonomy and its coherence within the context of Jamesian critical reflection – contains a veiled but detectable allusion to *Madame Bovary,* so as almost to project Isabel's story onto Emma's, and James's own experimenting with form onto his predecessor's.

"Isabel Archer was a young person of many theories; her imagination was remarkably active. . . . among her contemporaries she passed for a young woman of extraordinary profundity." "She only had a general idea that people were right when they treated her as if she were rather superior." "The girl had a certain nobleness of imagination which rendered her a good many services and played her a great many tricks." "Altogether, with her meagre knowledge, her inflated ideals, her confidence at once innocent and dogmatic, her temper at once exacting and indulgent, her mixture of curiosity and fastidiousness, of vivacity and indifference, her desire to look very well and to be if possible even better, her determination to see, to try, to know, her combination of the delicate, desultory, flame-like spirit and the eager and personal creature of conditions: she would be an easy victim of scientific criticism if she were not intended to awaken on the reader's part an impulse more tender and more purely expectant."[3] Such is the protagonist of *The Portrait of a Lady,* and this is why her vicissitudes are of interest: "She was intelligent and generous; it was a fine free nature; but what was she going to do with herself? This question was irregular, for with most women one had no occasion to ask it. Most women did with themselves nothing at all; they waited, in attitudes more or less gracefully passive, for a man to come that way and furnish them with a destiny. Isabel's originality was that she gave one an impression of having intentions of her own" (Chap. 7).

From this core, the story develops. A young American who has come to Europe with her aunt Mrs. Touchett to see, to know, and to experience life, Isabel Archer in her desire to preserve her independence refuses to marry either the English Lord Warburton or the American Caspar Goodwood. Isabel's seriously ill cousin Ralph, who is secretly and hopelessly in love with her, gives up his rather large paternal inheritance to her advantage: as a rich woman, Isabel will be able "to meet the requirements of [her] imagination" (Chap. 18). Her riches, however, lead Isabel into the trap of a fortune hunter, Gilbert Osmond, a refined and egocentric esthete and a widower with a daughter, Pansy. With the help of a common friend, Madame Merle, who introduces Osmond to Isabel precisely for the purpose, Osmond manages to charm Isabel into marrying him. After the wedding, Isabel discovers her husband's true nature and later comes to understand Mme. Merle's role in plotting the marriage: an ex-lover of Osmond's, she is Pansy's real mother. When she hears that Ralph is dying, Isabel leaves her home in Rome against her husband's will and rushes to England; Goodwood, whom she meets there, declares his love once again and urges her to leave Osmond. But two days later, when she appears to be on the verge of a final break with her husband, Isabel leaves England to return to Rome.

Because of its concrete references to social reality and its thematic richness, *The Portrait of a Lady* has been universally acclaimed even by those who criticize James's late works, and it has inspired countless critical studies bent on elucidating its various features. Several thematic motifs coalesce around the central problem — what will Isabel do with herself? Among them, the opposition between freedom and constraint is perhaps the most basic: Isabel's quest for freedom and independence paradoxically leads her to lock herself up in a house-prison. Beneath Isabel's error of judgment lies her contradictory idea of freedom.

In Chapter 19, Isabel and Mme. Merle have a "metaphysical" conversation, during which Mme. Merle states her notion of the self as a being which finds its expression in the exterior circumstances of life: " 'One's self — for other people — is one's expression of one's self; and one's house, one's furniture, one's garments, the books one reads, the company one keeps — these things are all expressive.' " In opposition to this conception of the relationship between the individual and circumstance, Isabel presents a version of the self as an isolated being having no relationship with external events: " 'I don't know whether I succeed in expressing myself, but I know that nothing else expresses me. Nothing that belongs to me is any measure of me; everything's on the contrary a limit, a barrier, and a perfectly arbitrary one.' " For Isabel the self is autonomous and not defined by its own decisions and external circumstances: but, precisely for this reason, such a self is free only when isolated, when lacking a role by which others could identify it. Thus, Isabel refuses to marry Warburton and Goodwood, each of whom she perceives to be "a collection of attributes" (Chap. 12), limited by social position and personal circumstances, and instead marries Osmond, who appears to her to be pure personality, having no specific social position and material circumstances to define or fix him. By becoming Osmond's wife, Isabel believes she will elude the fixedness of a definitive social role; instead she finds herself "ground in the very mill of the conventional" (Chap. 54).[4]

Furthermore, if choosing constrains – rather than expresses – the self, every choice becomes a limitation of one's infinite potential. By marrying Osmond, Isabel chooses to choose no more, to be released from making decisions over the use of her own money: "At bottom her money had been a burden, had been on her mind, which was filled with the desire to transfer the weight of it to some other conscience, to some more prepared receptacle. What would lighten her own conscience more effectually than to make it over to the man with the best taste in the world?" (Chap. 42) Paradoxically, it follows from Isabel's idea of self and freedom that only passivity can ensure freedom, since every action is a choice and, therefore, a limitation of one's self. Indeed, it is Isabel's imagination that is described as "active" from the very beginning. We witness mainly her *mental* activity, while her concrete actions and her very choices tend to be mostly negative and to reinforce her passivity: Isabel chooses *not* to marry Warburton, *not* to marry Goodwood, and to marry Osmond so as *not* to make any more decisions concerning her actions. It is only when she becomes aware of the deceit she has suffered, and of her own complicity in it, that Isabel makes some real decisions, such as going to England to see the dying Ralph. But then the nature of her final action remains utterly ambiguous: does going back to Osmond mark her decision to accept consciously the role in which she found herself to be trapped – thereby transforming deception into free choice (or, to be consistent, paying for her own mistake)? Or is it a flight from the responsibilities of the autonomous life she could still lead away from Osmond?

This freedom/constraint, activity/passivity antinomy and Isabel's tendency to confuse the two terms of the opposition find their best expression in the definition of happiness that Isabel gives to her friend Henrietta: "'A swift carriage, of a dark night, rattling with four horses over roads that one can't see – that's my idea of happiness'" (Chap. 17). This definition is a vision of utmost movement and activity, but that movement and activity are determined from outside and, therefore, coincide with the utmost passivity. Furthermore, Isabel's remark is reminiscent of one of Emma Bovary's fantasies (Henrietta's words, when she says that Isabel is speaking "'like the heroine of an immoral novel'" [Chap. 17], reinforce that echo)[5] and underlines one of the factors contributing to Isabel's error of judgment: her imagination has been nourished by novels and is full of ideals which do not always correspond to reality.

In *The Portrait of a Lady,* however, James develops this old theme in a completely new way. From Jane Austen's Catherine Morland to Flaubert's Emma Bovary, the "romantic" heroine's imagination had always exercised itself on love or marriage; in contrast, Isabel Archer's ideals concern independence from men and the fulfilling of her own personal potential. And, let us be sure to notice, James's irony (after all tempered by that "impulse more tender and more purely expectant" [Chap. 6], which he asks of his reader and which he himself feels for Isabel) is not applied to those ideals per se, but to Isabel's blindness in attempting to realize them in ways which conflict with them. Through this use of irony, James distances himself from the prevalent attitude among those writers who, responding to the debate stirred up by the rising women's movement, were tackling in their own writing the problem of women's independence. The prevailing narrative formula was this: an attractive girl who seeks independence falls in love, thereby realizes the falsity of her beliefs, and happily devotes herself to the true ends of a woman's life, marriage and children. W. D. Howells's *Dr. Breen's Practice* – which was published in installments in the *Atlantic Monthly* at the same time as *The Portrait of a Lady* – tells such a story: its heroine is a young doctor who gives up her practice, gets married, and makes use of her studies in an acceptable feminine way, by taking care of the workers in her husband's factory. We can measure the distance which separates James's novel from this formula simply by noticing that Isabel's marriage does not function as rescue; rather, it functions as capture and imprisonment.

While James develops the freedom/constraint theme mainly through Isabel's story, each of the other female characters in the novel introduces a different aspect of the problem and offers a different solution, thereby providing a term of comparison against which to measure the protagonist's personal quest. Mrs. Touchett has cut out a space for her autonomy within marriage by living separately from her husband, but at the cost of emotional detachment as well; while Mme. Merle, who has found her own autonomous social function as mistress of conventions and manipulator of appearances, is also a slave to this very role and must sacrifice her feelings to it. Henrietta is the emancipated American type, while Pansy allows her personality to disappear under the shadow of her father's will.

After all, we can read Isabel's story in an almost infinite number of ways, as the myriad critical interpretations of the novel indicate. For instance, much has been written about the peculiarly American characteristics of the protagonist and her outlook on life. Undoubtedly, Isabel's identity lies also in her national roots, to the point that we could say of her what Agostino Lombardo says of James: neither "would be conceivable without that exploration of conscience, that ethical rigor, that almost exclusive attention to the problems of the human soul which are peculiar to a culture born out of Puritanism, a culture in which even the transcendentalist revolution assimilated Puritan themes."[6] It is in this cultural climate that a character such as Isabel Archer is born; and her story is also an initiation story – an extremely fruitful theme in American literature – which takes on a typically Jamesian quality because of its international character.

One final remark, among the many possible ones, is that money in this novel (as in all others by James) is shown to be the hidden driving force behind social and personal relations. This observation in itself suffices to refute the legend of a James who was stingy with "concrete" details simply because he was incapable − by virtue of personal and social limitations − of understanding the importance of such details and noting their presence in ordinary life.[7]

In *The Portrait of a Lady* there is all this and more. Paradoxically, however, this novel, whose referential physicality and concreteness − typical features of the nineteenth-century realistic novel − stand out against the "abstract" nature of James's late works, is also the work in which James posits the nonexistence of "facts" as objective entities and, therefore, implicitly affirms the need to revise radically the notion of realism and the existing relationship between the novel and reality.

Quite explicitly, the starting point of *The Portrait of a Lady* is neither a story nor a situation which promises to develop, but, as the Preface tells us, a character and her awareness: not her adventures, but "her sense of them, her sense *for* them." James thus devalues the traditional concept of story (*fabula*) as a series of significant actions and events linked together: what would have been crucial moments in other texts − dramatic turning points such as Isabel's departure from America, her wedding, the birth and death of her son − appear only in retrospective summaries; they are not dramatized and shown to the reader. We know of Isabel's final departure for Rome, the climax and dénouement of the story, only from a secondary character's curt remark. Likewise, scenes (i.e., dramatized events) tend to be repetitive and to reiterate only a few fundamental patterns: confrontation of ideas, courting, and deception. The same can be said of settings. With the single exception of a square in London and the monuments in Rome, the entire novel − which nevertheless does tell of travels in Europe and around the world − is set in a few gardens and houses: Isabel's grandmother's in Albany (only in retrospective scenes); Gardencourt, the Touchetts' house; Lockleigh, Lord Warburton's estate; the Crescentini palace, Mrs. Touchett's Florentine house; Osmond's house in Florence; and the Roccanera palace in Rome, where Isabel and Osmond live.

The same situations then repeat themselves incessantly so as to underline the notion that we should not look for development and transformation in the events themselves, but in levels of awareness and points of view. The truly dramatic turning points have to do with awareness, as in Isabel's long contemplative vigil which takes up all of Chapter 42 and which – James writes in his Preface – "throws the action further forward than twenty 'incidents' might have done" and is "a supreme illustration of the general plan."

"Action" has little to do with facts; rather, it concerns shifting and alternating points of view, the subjectivity of which is the only available reality, since objects exist only as seen by someone. And this discovery, which anticipates the epistemological relativism of much twentieth-century philosophy and literature, is at the heart of both theme and technique in *The Portrait of a Lady*. External reality does not exist on its own and cannot, therefore, be the object of narrative; the only existing reality is the inner one, which transacts extremely subtle exchanges with the external one. There is no *one* reality, no *one* appearance, but there are many different points of view. Isabel's desire is that "she would be what she appeared, and she would appear what she was" (Chap. 6), but one's identity for others is always necessarily framed by their gazes as well as by one's own point of view. And since the same is true of the reality of others in one's own eyes, every deception – such as the one leading to Isabel's marriage – is always also self-deception. Above all, identity is a way of looking at life; freedom is being allowed one's own point of view ("'the privilege of the weakest and humblest of us,'" writes Isabel to Warburton, [Chap. 13]); marriage is an exchange, an identification, or an expropriation of points of view. Warburton asks Isabel to marry him and, therefore, "to see something of his system from his own point of view" (Chap. 12); she refuses because, she explains, "'we see our lives from our own point of view; . . . and I shall never be able to see mine in the manner you proposed'" (Chap. 13). Isabel marries Osmond to share what she thinks is his point of view, believing that marriage with him can lead her "to the high places of happiness, from which the world would seem to lie below one, so that one could look down with a sense of exaltation and advantage" (Chap. 42). And, finally, it is precisely Isabel's identity, as expressed

41

from her own point of view, which provokes her husband's hatred of her: "She had a certain way of looking at life which he took as a personal offence" (Chap. 42).

In the world of the novel, eyes and gazes are just as important as words in establishing relationships and exploring situations: each character is a spectator and a spectacle in relation to the others; nevertheless, it is mostly on Isabel that the other characters' gazes, and the reader's, focus, and it is mostly through her eyes (her way of looking at life, that is, her mind) that the reader perceives the reality surrounding her. Theme and technique, then, are one: *The Portrait of a Lady* is a novel of and about point of view, focused as it is on Isabel's consciousness and, only when their points of view help to "locate" and illustrate the protagonist, on those of her "satellites." Both subject and object of observation, Isabel reveals her self as she reveals the world.

This is the "limited point of view" technique: a narrative, not necessarily in the first person, is nevertheless filtered through a character's gaze and consciousness so that external reality exists only as refracted in the mind of what James calls the "vessel of consciousness" or "reflector." The narrator's task is to present a character's consciousness without using the character's words, representing, that is, as if in a dramatic scene, not actions, but a mind. While he is the one to have theorized this technique (which other novelists, including Flaubert, had used, but only occasionally), James does not apply it dogmatically, especially in *The Portrait of a Lady*. For this novel's shifting of points of view — that is, the movement, skillfully disguised by the voice of the narrator, from the consciousness of one character to another — is the central means of ensuring variety to a novel otherwise lacking, as mentioned above, the traditional kind of "action" which would hold the reader's attention.[8]

Theme and technique, then, constantly refer to one another and, thereby, confirm that the text is self-enclosed, autonomous, and self-sufficient in relation to what is external to it. This closure is, of course, reinforced by the title: *Portrait* alludes to an enclosed form, which the frame ostensibly isolates from the surrounding reality and which, in the novel, constitutes a completely formal principle of intrinsic unity, arbitrarily chosen by the author to circumscribe his subject and in no way dependent on verisimilitude or external referents. A portrait is modeled on a real person, but the novel is modeled on the portrait, an artistic object in its own right, and within its own frame it *creates*– it does not imitate – the object of representation, thereby freeing itself completely from mimesis. In other words, the portrait, and not the person, is the principle of unity for the novel. In a radical transgression of traditional novelistic models, *The Portrait of a Lady* achieves its closure – the completion of the portrait – without bringing the protagonist's biography to its finish; it ends, as a matter of fact, in an absolutely and enigmatically open-ended situation. In this particular case, the reader, an outsider to Isabel's consciousness, does not know what motivates her departure, so that the silence and the void behind it become filled with hypotheses but can never finally be deciphered. The novel does not find its meaning and unity in life – which is open-ended, chaotic, and meaningless – but in art, in form. The novel's reality and realism consist of creating an autonomous and fictitious microcosm, a double, not an imitation, of the world.

The portrait also functions, not simply as a principle of unity and a guarantee of self-sufficiency, but as a compositional model which governs the text on all levels. Centered on a character, and not a story, *The Portrait of a Lady* is, like a portrait, static and not dynamic; it works on the principle of expansion, not of transformation; it illustrates and clarifies data already present from the very beginning – that is, Isabel and her personality. Subsequent episodes do not change her nature; rather, they are consequences of it, they illustrate it, they illuminate its details, they disclose it to Isabel herself and to us. And, in so doing, they bring about the novel's only transformation: the shift from consciousness to awareness. As we shall see, Isabel's story is already fully contained in her first appearance in the narrative discourse (at Gardencourt in Chapter 2) as well as in the story (at the house in Albany before her meeting with Mrs. Touchett). Likewise, the compositional method of the novel is already contained, miniaturized as it were, in its opening sentence, which is entirely governed by the inclusion of every element in a broader one and by the movement from the general to the particular: "Under certain circumstances there are few hours in life more agreeable than the hour dedicated to the ceremony known as afternoon tea" (Chap. 1). And the first long paragraph also moves with regularity from the general (the ceremony of afternoon tea) to the particular (this specific afternoon tea, the weather and the time, the characters who are present) and finally focuses on the house, the center of this first picture, which prepares us for, and serves as background to, Isabel's appearance.[9]

"Under certain circumstances": the novel opens with a limitation, the establishment of a boundary; and, while referring to the enclosed form of the portrait and the enclosed structure of the novel, this delimitation, this closure, also posits itself as the central signifier to which all levels of the text conform. Isabel's story is fundamentally a story of closure, the story of an illusory opening and of increasing suffocation. As already mentioned, the whole novel unfolds in houses and gardens, and these apparently "neutral" and purely denotative — but actually connotating and connotative — settings can be analyzed as important elements of the novel's meaning.

In the novel, all spaces are enclosed, circumscribed, including public and open spaces (such as the square in London — an enclosure, a "quadrangle of dusky houses" [Chap. 15]) and gardens. The Gardencourt garden (whose name already inscribes its ambiguous nature as open space—enclosure) has a "carpet of turf" which "seemed but the extension of a luxurious interior," "a shade as dense as that of velvet curtains," and is "furnished, like a room" (Chap. 1) with chairs and rugs. Isabel makes her first appearance on the threshold between the house and this enclosed garden; she moves towards the open space, whose freedom, however, is illusory: what appears to be an opening reasserts closure. And Isabel will end her quest where she started it: the Roccanera palace (whose name is telling: black fortress) has a dark, cold, and suffocating interior, like that of the house in Albany where Isabel would sit, both as a child and in the beginning of the story, knowing that beyond the room's bolted doors and windows there was a street, but refusing to look outside because "this would have interfered with her theory that there was a strange, unseen place on the other side" (Chap. 3), a place conceived by turns as a scene of delight or terror. Isabel deceives herself, and her imagination causes her to confuse closure with opening and to desire both at the same time. Her "desire for unlimited expansion" (Chap. 35) – which makes her reject Warburton's and Goodwood's marriage proposals – leads her to marry Osmond, whom she perceives as "a man living in the open air of the world," only to find "the infinite vista of a multiplied life to be a dark, narrow alley with a dead wall at the end" (Chap. 42). Isabel's journey ends against this dead wall, in the prison of "the house of darkness" (Chap. 42). This defeat, nevertheless, corresponds to the protagonist's highest degree of awareness, a paradox which emphasizes the schism between the story of consciousness and the story of action.[10]

The connotative function of elements which appear to be purely referential provides us with an excellent example of the subtle correspondences among the different levels of the text. Like the spatial elements (houses, gardens, doors, windows), environmental ones, such as light and darkness, cold and heat, are not simply neutral information producing the effect of realism, but rather connotative vehicles of meaning which, as pure images, function as parts of rich clusters of metaphors. Countless metaphors run through the whole novel (a feature which will characterize James's late works); among them, houses and gardens constitute perhaps what is the most conspicuous group, both quantitatively and qualitatively. To cite only a few examples, Isabel is a well-proportioned building in Ralph's eyes, and a garden in her own: "her nature had, in her conceit, a certain garden-like quality . . . which made her feel that introspection was, after all, an exercise in the open air" (Chap. 6) (and here we notice yet another instance of the confusion between interiors and exteriors, closures and openings, which lies at the root of Isabel's error of judgment). In Chapter 42, while meditating on her relationship with Osmond, Isabel describes her husband's original intention in the following terms: "Her mind was to be his – attached to his own like a small garden-plot to a deer-park." And finally, "the house of darkness, the house of dumbness, the house of suffocation," into which Isabel's marriage has turned, is completely metaphorical.

Furthermore, the metaphor of the house stands out in the Preface, creating a complex and important correspondence between every level of the novel and its global structure (*The Portrait of a Lady,* James tells us, is "a square and spacious house," built brick by brick, "a literary monument," "a structure reared with an 'architectural' competence"), and also between this novel and the novel as genre. The latter is, according to the now famous definition in James's Preface, a "house of fiction" whose countless windows — each one offering a point of view to the observer, that is, "the consciousness of the artist" — open up onto "the human scene." In a telescopic fashion, then, the relativity of point of view involves the author as well as the characters: what sense can it make to speak of a novel as "true to reality," if there are as many realities as there are novelists?

The presence on different levels of houses and points of view establishes a complex game of correspondences and relationships between the world of the story and the world of narrative discourse. Likewise, the compositional model of the portrait which governs the narrative is reinforced in the story by numerous paintings, galleries, and comparisons of objects or people to paintings — not to mention the great number of allusions to "the novel" as a filter and a term of comparison for the world in Isabel's mind, to the point that she even perceives herself as a character in a novel caught in a novel-like situation. *The Portrait of a Lady,* then, weaves a dense web of references to itself and to its internal composition. And these self-reflexive references — the novel's dialogue with itself and its thematizing itself, thereby inaugurating the inclusion of a discourse *on* the text *within* the text itself — make *The Portrait of a Lady* decisively modern. As a novel which, in its discovery of the central importance of point of view, radically questions the possibility and the very concept of a traditionally mimetic narrative, and which, by promoting the reader's awareness of form, reorients the reader's attention away from "the world" to art, *The Portrait of a Lady* marks a crucial moment not only in James's artistic itinerary, but also in the history of the novel as literary form.

NOTES

1. Jean Rousset, *Forme et signification. Essais sur les structures littéraires de Corneille à Claudel* (Paris: Librairie José Corti, 1962).

2. Jonathan Culler has thoroughly analyzed the workings of these strategies in *Flaubert: The Uses of Uncertainty* (Ithaca: Cornell University Press, 1974). [*Translator's note:* Izzo makes use of Gérard Genette's terminology throughout the essay. I have, therefore, translated *racconto* (*récit*) as "narrative" and "narrative discourse" and *storia* (*histoire*, Propp's *fabula*) as "story." Izzo's distinction between focalization and voice and her use of the terms *scena* (scene) and *sommario* (summary) later in the essay are also from Genette's *Figures III* (Paris: Editions du Seuil, 1972), a portion of which was translated by Jane E. Lewin as *Narrative Discourse: An Essay in Method* (Ithaca: Cornell University Press, 1980).]

3. Henry James, *The Portrait of a Lady*, ed. Robert D. Bamberg (New York: Norton, 1975), Chap. 6. All further references are to this edition and are included parenthetically in the text.

4. For an exhaustive discussion of Isabel's notion of self, see Tony Tanner, "The Fearful Self: Henry James's *The Portrait of a Lady*," *Critical Quarterly* 7 (1965): 205–19, and Donald L. Mull, "Freedom and Judgment: The Antinomy of Action in *The Portrait of a Lady*," *Arizona Quarterly* (Summer 1971): 124–32.

5. This point is convincingly made by Adeline R. Tintner, "Isabel's Carriage-Image and Emma's Daydream," *Modern Fiction Studies* (Summer 1976): 227–31.

6. Agostino Lombardo, Introduction to Henry James, *Le Prefazioni* (Venezia: Neri Pozza, 1956), p. xlv. Tony Tanner, "The Fearful Self," also stresses the specifically American quality of Isabel's self.

7. For a reading of the novel that emphasizes the problematic relation between the aesthetic and the economic both in the text and in James's theory of representation, see Edgar A. Dryden, "The Image in the Mirror: The Double Economy of James's *Portrait*," *Genre* 13, no. 1 (Spring 1980): 31–49.

8. A detailed account of shifts in point of view and of the narrator's varying degrees of presence in the novel is provided by Martha Collins, "The Narrator, the Satellites, and Isabel Archer: Point of View in *The Portrait of a Lady*," *Studies in the Novel* 8 (1976): 142–57.

9. For a careful analysis of the first paragraph of *Portrait*, see Catherine Rihoit, "Waiting for Isabel: An Analysis of the Levels of Significance

in the First Fifteen Sentences of *The Portrait of a Lady*," in André Joly and Thomas K. H. Fraser, eds., *Studies in English* (Lille: Université de Lille III, 1975), pp. 187–225.

10. Illuminating comments on space in the novel are provided by R. W. Stallman, "The Houses That James Built – *The Portrait of a Lady*," *The Texas Quarterly* (Winter 1958): 176–96.

The Fatherless Heroine and the Filial Son: Deep Background for *The Portrait of a Lady*

ALFRED HABEGGER

AMONG the many ways of summing up Isabel Osmond's earlier life there is one that goes like this:

The late Mr. Archer, indulgent and affectionate, provided his favorite daughter with numerous advantages, the chief of which was not to bring her up too strictly. But he was somewhat irresponsible, and once, when Isabel was in her eleventh year (thirteenth in the serial version), he left her in Switzerland with a French maid, who then ran off with a Russian. A sturdy adventurer even then, the girl was quite certain there was no cause to worry or feel deserted.

Now in her early twenties, her father having died, Isabel has grown up to be a remarkably independent young woman who seems ready and eager to take on the world. Only, for the time being, she has secluded herself in a remote room of the same house where her father died. She is undergoing a harsh Prussian discipline, forcing her mind "to advance, to halt, to retreat."[1] Mostly retreat, it would seem, for while "the large number of those to whom he owed money" feel that Mr. Archer got what he deserved in his early, unhappy death, Isabel naively worships the "handsome, much-loved father. . . . It was a great good fortune to have been his daughter; Isabel was even proud of her parentage" (Chap. 4).

At Gardencourt Isabel is lively and alert and appears to have outlived her bereavement, but she is still wearing black — "more than a year" (Chap. 2) after Mr. Archer's death. (Later, after her child dies, she discards her mourning within six months [Chap. 39].) When Ralph Touchett makes a joke about her adoption by his mother, he seems to touch a nerve and the young woman briefly loses her composure: "'Adopted me?' The girl stared, and her blush came back to her, together with a momentary look of pain, which gave her interlocutor some alarm. He had underestimated the effect of his words. . . . 'Oh, no; she has not adopted me,' she said. 'I am not a candidate for adoption'" (Chap. 2). Obviously, she must have it understood that she will remain in charge of her life. But what does that momentary look of pain signify?

Months later, in Chapter 24, visiting Gilbert Osmond's apartments on Bellosguardo for the first time, Isabel is fascinated by his obedient, porcelain-like daughter. Pansy is fifteen years old and physically mature (Chap. 35) but somehow remains a little girl. Isabel is twenty-two. Osmond is forty. They are all sitting together. Suddenly, the devoted father does something: he has Pansy get up "out of her chair, . . . making her stand between his knees, leaning against him while he passed his arm round her little waist. The child fixed her eyes on Isabel with a still, disinterested gaze, which seemed void of an intention, but conscious of an attraction." The silent display has no heat or pressure, only a cool, still limpidity: a childish grown-up is required, in the presence of a stranger, to stand between her father's knees, her waist encircled by his arm, her mind emptied of all volition or interest and containing only a passive responsiveness. The eyes of the child-woman are wide open, but she doesn't seem to be fully awake. We wonder, what cruel operation has been performed on her to make her so perfectly responsive to another's will? Is the will that has shaped her engaged in another project at this very moment? Could Osmond be using Pansy to reach Isabel in some sinister fashion?

It seems so, for when we next observe father and daughter in this scene, standing now but still entwined, the heroine has begun to mimic the feelings that presumably possess the serene daughter:

> Mr. Osmond stood there . . . with his hands in the pockets of his jacket, and his daughter, who had now locked her arm into one of his own, clinging to him and looking up, while her eyes moved from his own face to Isabel's. Isabel waited, with a certain unuttered contentedness, to have her movements directed.

Again, though there is not the slightest hint of applied force, the father appears to be in total control. He doesn't even have to use his hands. Pansy seemingly takes the initiative of clinging, locking to him, and mysteriously, Isabel has begun to want to do the same, despite her insistence not too long before that she was not a candidate for adoption. She too would like to be a passive daughter, and she feels a novel embarrassment about her undirected independence: "I am rather ashamed of my plans; I make a new one every day." Something tells her she is not at all the right sort of woman.

The courtship begins. Since we have already witnessed the scene in which Madame Merle offers Isabel to Osmond, we are anxious to know how the young woman will regard him. We soon find out, in Chapter 26:

> She liked to think of him. She had carried away an image from her visit to his hill-top which her subsequent knowledge of him did nothing to efface and which happened to take her fancy particularly – the image of a quiet, clever, sensitive, distinguished man, strolling on a moss-grown terrace above the sweet Val d'Arno, and holding by the hand a little girl whose sympathetic docility gave a new aspect to childhood. The picture was not brilliant, but she liked its lowness of tone, and the atmosphere of summer twilight that pervaded it. It seemed to tell a story – a story of the sort that touched her most easily; to speak of a serious choice . . . ; of a lonely, studious life in a lovely land; of an old sorrow . . . ; a feeling of pride . . . ; a care for beauty and perfection . . . a quaint, half-anxious, half-helpless fatherhood.

The young woman's fancy has been taken captive by a resonant and compelling image. She isn't in love yet, doesn't know what it feels like to desire another person. She has simply seen – been shown – a picture she can't get out of her mind, a picture of a father and his daughter. She likes to think about this picture, to return to it as one savors a pleasing daydream or rereads a favorite passage in a novel. She has found – or been handed – a kind of fetish, one that seems "to tell a story." The phrases lightly sketching in this story have the amplified organ-tones of a certain kind of fiction – "lonely, studious life," "old sorrow." Vague in plot, the story nevertheless evokes a strong emotional response and carries a special and distinguished aura. A choice dream has magically come to life before the eyes of the free American girl. She isn't in the dream, of course, for the simple reason that she isn't distinguished. She's not like the refined man and the docile girl. *He* would never abandon her in her eleventh year. *She* would never be restless. They don't change their plans every day. How comforting just to finger the quiet picture they make.

But why is the father so sad, half-anxious, half-helpless? Is there something he needs that the fond dreamer might be able to contribute? Is there a way for the dreamer to get into the dream? "I should like to see you when you are tired and satiated," Osmond says to her. "I shall prefer you in that state" (Chap. 29).

1

After surveying his contemporaries' comments on James's fiction, Linda J. Taylor observes that *The Portrait* "made him famous all across the [American] continent. . . . It was James's most widely reviewed work and created a peak in his reputation."[2] The most detailed record of a reader's contemporary response to the novel is in Constance Fenimore Woolson's February 12, 1882, letter to the author. By turns fulsome and resentful, this letter gave special attention to the spectacle of Osmond and Pansy and to Isabel's responsive fancy. Noting how Osmond poses with "his little daughter, in her short white frock," Woolson lavished praise on James's rendition of Isabel's captivated imagination: "And then the impression summed up in chapter 26 – page 242 – how perfectly one understands the effect – sees what she saw, feels what she felt. It was precisely the sort of picture to win an Isabel. And it almost seemed to me as if you were the only man who has ever divined it."[3] This obliquely confessional passage, with its rather coy substitution of the impersonal "one" for "I," shows how profoundly James's exhibition of Isabel's fantasy life could speak to a contemporary woman reader. James had not invented, he had "divined," this fantasy life, and Woolson became almost abject in registering her shock of recognition.

James's reply, if he wrote one, is not extant. His one surviving comment on the effect that Osmond and his daughter have on Isabel's imagination is to be found in his 1914 memoir, *Notes of a Son and Brother,* where he acknowledges that he himself had been inspired by the picture of two friends, Francis Boott and his daughter Lizzie, in their Florentine villa:

> A not other than lonely and bereft American, addicted to the arts and endowed for them, housed to an effect of long expatriation in a massive old Florentine villa with a treasured and tended little daughter by his side, *that* was the germ which for reasons beyond my sounding the case of Frank Boott had been appointed to plant deep down in my vision of things.[4]

Like the Preface to *The Portrait,* this passage appears to reveal a private source of inspiration, but in fact the door James opens merely discloses another door that remains closed. The Bootts furnished James with his image — fine. But why did the image make such an impression on him? "For reasons beyond my sounding." James, dreaming up *The Portrait* long ago, here seems almost as helplessly responsive as Isabel is. He liked to dwell on a certain vision, and he had (or has) no idea why. His use of the passive voice — "had been appointed" — even hints that some external agency had been directing his imagination, much as Osmond directs the heroine's.

One possible reason why the father-daughter image gripped Isabel, and James, *and* Woolson, is that it was a resonant *public* image of the time, especially for novel-readers. Isabel was the heroine of a thousand novels, the independent orphan-heroine in search of the sorrowing father-lover. Neither the momentary look of pain nor the image that seems to tell a story was original with *The Portrait.* Both belonged to a type of heroine and to a nineteenth-century story-formula containing her. Osmond is the paternal lover who already has a daughter — like Mr. Lloyd in Catharine Sedgwick's *New-England Tale* (1822) or Rochester in *Jane Eyre* (1847). Isabel is the girl who suddenly finds herself in an unprotected state, who is forced to take care of herself after her father dies or in some other way deserts her, and who often finds consolation in the end by marrying this same poor lost father. She resembles the heroines of Susan Warner's *The Wide, Wide World* (1851) and *Queechy* (1852), Augusta J. Evans's *Beulah* (1859), Adeline Whitney's *Faith Gartney's Girlhood* (1863), and Louisa May Alcott's "The Marble Woman; or, The Mysterious Model" (1865). But there are differences, chiefly because Isabel is a metaheroine as well as a heroine. That is, *The Portrait* does tell the traditional orphan-heroine's story, but it also is concerned to enclose, sum up, assess this story. W. D. Howells pointed out in his perceptive 1882 essay on James that unlike George Eliot's Dorothea Brooke, who has "grand aims," Isabel has "beautiful dreams,"[5] and this distinction hints at the critical nature of James's narrative, which is *about* the treacherous feminine imagination that had created a vast Anglo-American tradition of fiction.

In the American 1850s, when James grew to be a passionate reader, the heroine of almost all the most popular novels was a girl, frequently a little girl, whose sudden homelessness required her to look after herself. She inevitably matured with amazing rapidity, learning how to provide her own livelihood, acquiring leverage over those who were older and more powerful, and resolving terrible moral dilemmas all by herself and even settling one or two riddles of the ages as she went. But she often fell secretly in love with the man of the house where she happened to be residing, or with the preceptor who kindly supervised her education, or with a strong, older, manly, unmarried minister or doctor, and in the end she married this masterly guardian. Most of the novels do not seem to be conscious of the contradiction between the juvenile dependency her final union implies and her preceding hard-won independence.

During the Civil War a younger and more anxious generation of American women novelists tried to work out the contradictions and dilemmas of what Nina Baym has called "woman's fiction."[6] In James's first year as a professional writer, he reviewed three of the most daring novels by these younger writers – Anne Moncure Crane's *Emily Chester,* Louisa May Alcott's *Moods,* and Elizabeth Stoddard's *Two Men.* All three focused on the tormented relationship between a remarkably original and self-reliant girl and a strong older man. It was precisely the treatment of this material that aroused James's youthful ire. His unpublished notice of *Two Men* sarcastically observed that its romance between a girl and a "middle-aged man" was "quite after the actual taste." With *Emily Chester*, he noted that Max Crampton "is the repetition of a type that has of late years obtained great favor with lady novelists: the ugly, rich, middle-aged lover." With *Moods* the young man's disdain overflowed: "We are utterly weary of stories about precocious little girls. . . . They are always the precursors of a . . . middle-aged lover." James had a deep hatred for this quiet, understated tyrant, who "spends his time in breaking the hearts and the wills of demure little school-girls,"[7] and he couldn't understand why so many heroines and women novelists let themselves be browbeaten by him. Other reviewers frequently objected to heroes of the Rochester type, but James seems to have felt a special animus, as if he had seen a particularly chilling example of disguised paternalistic oppression from very close up, or had himself struggled against it.

What James attempted in his first published long narrative, *Watch and Ward* (1871), was to purify this disturbing story about the precocious girl and her middle-aged lover. The novel begins when the irresponsible Mr. Lambert shoots himself, thus abandoning both his debts and his little girl, Nora — much as Mr. Archer has abandoned Isabel, first in Switzerland and then by dying. Kind Roger Lawrence, who lives on a patrimony and travels to Peru if not all over the world (as James had accused the middle-aged lover of doing), pities the miserably orphaned child and tries to comfort her:

> "Do you remember my taking you last night in my arms?" It was his fancy that, for an answer, she faintly blushed. He laid his hand on her head and smoothed away her thick disordered hair. She submitted to his consoling touch with a plaintive docility. He put his arm round her waist. An irresistible sense of her childish sweetness, of her tender feminine promise, stole softly into his pulses.[8]

How suggestive the passage is, especially if we look ahead to Osmond's use of Pansy's waist, or to the way Isabel looks to him for comfort after losing her own father. Is little twelve-year-old Nora in the same danger that Isabel and Pansy will be? *Of course not,* the whole narrative insists. Roger is decent and liberal, *kind, kind, kind,* as the stage version of Christopher Newman would proclaim himself to be. Roger gives Nora perfect freedom to choose, and if he hopes all the while that she will choose to satisfy *his* pulses by eventually marrying him, he staunchly refuses to force her choice.

But *Watch and Ward* was in most respects a failure. It couldn't be published as a book until James's later novels created a market, and its representation of life violated some of James's most vigorously expressed convictions. Five years earlier, reviewing Adeline Whitney's *The Gayworthys,* he had showed great indignation at those narratives (such as Thackeray's *Henry Esmond*) that grounded erotic love in attachments originating in childhood: "if we desire to learn the various circumstances under which lovemaking may be conducted, let us not repair to the nursery and the school-room. . . . The age for Daphnis and Chloe has passed. Passion and sentiment must always be more or less intelligent not to shock the public taste."[9] It was James's objective in *Watch and Ward* to produce a fully conscious – "intelligent" – representation of nursery lovemaking, yet in spite of the fact that the novel concerns the adult's feeling for the child more than the child's for the adult, it finally conveys the same sense of perverse innocence as the fiction James had criticized. Roger glides with suspicious ease from Nora's "childish sweetness" to her "tender feminine promise." Then there's his Humbert Humbert–like question about "last night in my arms." These and other glaring ambiguities in the novel derive from the problematic nature of the task James had set himself – providing a refined version of the vulgar guardian-ward romance. Instead of expressing his own strong anger at the middle-aged lover, James was somewhat foolishly seeking to rehabilitate him.

For James, the logical step after the pretty-pretty *Watch and Ward* was to provide his next orphan-heroine with both a puerile love for a father figure and an independent source of income and *then* see what she would do. The fact that James took this step in *The Portrait,* however, does not mean he was merely continuing his earlier, misguided enterprise of purifying women's fiction. It would have been captious for him to continue hammering away at the women's genre, even if that was where the vitality and much of the market lay, and it would have been opportunistic to override his own masculine sense of the servility in much feminine fiction. The decisive turn of mind that eventuated in *The Portrait* was a final impatience with women novelists. If all the precociously independent heroines would insist on falling for a middle-aged monster, all right then, his own heroine would do so with a vengeance. And if it was not possible to renovate the old masterly lover, then he should be made as quiet and sinister and poisonous as possible.

Hence James worked out his most ambitious novel to date precisely by developing – not eliminating – the falsities in the genre it belonged to. He refused to take at face value either the benevolent distinction of the middle-aged lover or the heroine's proclaimed love of liberty. Let her sense of freedom weigh on her so heavily that she begins to dream of confinement, of daughterly surrender.[10] Restore the purse that Nora loses at the end of *Watch and Ward*, or better, have some unexpected inheritance be the very thing that causes the heroine's true nature to declare itself, so that a hidden internal bondage subverts her gloriously untrammeled ideal. And shouldn't there be a generous friend who naively believes in her independence (for James himself had been this person while reading Crane's *Opportunity* and while writing *Watch and Ward*), someone whose hopefulness only ensures the heroine's self-entrapment?

It is because *The Portrait* resisted the premise that the heroine truly wishes to be free that the novel picked up and revised so many hallmarks of women's fiction, from Crane's three novels in particular. Crane's first heroine, Emily Chester, had roundly declared: "If I were to marry, I should die, I should suffocate! . . . I have lived a free life too long, not to revolt from the very shadow of a chain! . . . It is the aim of my existence to become a self-contained, self-sufficing woman, depending on myself for happiness."[11] Isabel Archer says the same thing, the difference being that her creator nudges the reader toward a recognition of the spread-eagle oratory. James's implication is that her noble resolution not to marry is stagy and unfelt: "'I like my liberty too much. If there is a thing in the world that I am fond of,' Isabel went on, with a slight recurrence of the grandeur that had shown itself a moment before − 'it is my personal independence'" (Chap. 16). At twenty-two Isabel is older than Harvey in *Opportunity* and the other precocious heroines, yet she retains her adolescent callowness. "Her thoughts were a tangle of vague outlines" (Chap. 6) in the book, and in the serial "her head was full of premature convictions and unproportioned images."[12]

In reviewing *Emily Chester*, James showed strong disdain for the heroine's calm stateliness. The author, he believed, had wished to create a "perfect" woman who would be "high-toned, high-spirited, high-souled," and he couldn't help belittling the heroine's pretensions: "when anything particularly disagreeable happens, she becomes very pale and calm and statuesque."[13] Isabel would be much the same. She insists on holding her head high long after her marriage has failed, has an a priori "nobleness of imagination," and feels "an unquenchable desire to think well of herself" (Chap. 6). Her wish to be always in the right represents her author's reinterpretation of Emily's perfection, and indeed of a whole line of women's heroines. The grandeur is generic; what James adds is the skeptical perspective that calls attention to the absurdity of Isabel's claim of superiority. In Chapter 34, where Ralph criticizes her fiancé, in the process giving Isabel her most disagreeable moment to date, she rebuffs him by taking a "heroic line" and maintaining an air of "careful calmness." The dignified composure slips from time to time, but it fools her into thinking she is being rather magnanimous to her poor misguided cousin. In the end, Ralph is chilled by his failure to make contact with her, and *she* feels exalted. This, one of James's finest scenes, reflects his canny sense of the noble nickel-plated mask worn by so many women's heroines of the time.

This scene exhibits another of Isabel's aspects that James took from *Emily Chester* and its congeners − the imperviousness of a theoretical emotion. One reason James detested Crane's first novel was that he regarded the heroine's passion as wholly unreal, something cooked up for the sake of "a theory" and then passed off as honest feeling. Although this view distorts Emily's situation, it applies beautifully to Isabel. There is so much infatuated nonsense in her system, as when she tells Warburton she can't marry him because to do so would be to try to escape her fate, that it's hard to believe she could possibly reestablish contact with her spontaneous feelings. (Of course, the point is that she can do so only at the cost of terrible pain brought on by her own blindness.) She has just enough insight into herself to fear she has lost "the natural and reasonable emotions of life" (Chap. 13), but she quickly dismisses this thought. Similarly, in Chapter 42, when she wonders whether she married "on a factitious theory," she blushes and tries to forget the shocking truth. The theory-thick approach to life, which James detected in Crane and other women novelists, is shown to be an all but inescapable slough.

Then there is Isabel's need for a master, a need harking back to the precocious girl who (in James's review of Alcott's *Moods*) says "Yes, sir" and "No, sir" to the middle-aged lover. In *The American* (1877) Christopher Newman's naive dream of freeing the perfect European woman from her ancient entanglements had been frustrated by her preference for the discipline of convent walls. *The Portrait,* in one sense a spin-off, had as its original working title *The Americana.*[14] Its protagonist, the "perfect" American heroine who loudly announces her freedom, would finally choose a similar form of confinement for herself, and again the walls would be palace walls and convent walls. But there are differences: *The Portrait's* convent is not so much a female refuge from worldly pressures as an indoctrination center that does the work of willful tyrants, in Pansy's case transforming an irregularly conceived child into a model girl-woman. Behind those walls Pansy has been "impregnated with the idea of submission, which was due to any one who took the tone of authority" (Chap. 22). "Impregnated" — the word tells us that *The Portrait's* convent offers a far less effective retreat from the world than the one Claire de Cintré chooses. Pansy's tampered-with mind is now "void of an intention" but "conscious of an attraction" as her daddy poses with her. The fact that Isabel's lively mind is captivated by the appallingly tractable Pansy sums up James's muted lesson: even the freest American woman dreams of submission to a dominating master.

It's well to remember that during the months James's plans for *The Portrait* became sufficiently firm to be mentioned in letters to Howells at the *Atlantic*, James admitted to his brother, William, that *Daniel Deronda* was "a great *exposé* of the female mind."[15] Juliet McMaster is one of several readers who argue that Isabel is drawn to the opposite of freedom – "death, and immobility, and suffering."[16] Sandra K. Fischer follows R. W. Stallman, William Bysshe Stein, and others in arguing that Isabel is repressed and prefers enclosed security to passion: "What Caspar shows Isabel at the end in a flash of illumination is that vulgar street – what she might call the base or common passions – and it confirms her in her terror."[17] These reactions originate in the daughter's abandonment. Because Isabel feels much more deserted by her father than she realizes, she is dangerously responsive to the studied self-portrait of the mutually dependent father and daughter. Freedom and fatherlessness have split the heroine into two disconnected halves – a partly factitious determination to be her own master and a dark fascination with images of dominance and submission. That is why she abruptly begins to imitate a fifteen-year-old girl's devotion to a forty-year-old father's every whim, and then takes him as her preceptor. "'You know everything, and I know nothing'" (Chap. 29).

Thus, embedded in the first thirty-five chapters of *The Portrait* is a certain grim thesis about the cause of the subjection of women. While not an exposé in tone of "the female mind," these chapters are emphatically an exposé in substance, as Woolson recognized. According to the Preface, written in 1906, the compositional problems that exercised James involved questions of substance much less than questions of presentation – especially the difficulty of getting the reader to sympathize with the "mere slim shade of an intelligent but presumptuous girl."[18] His basic problem was *not* how to build a lengthy narrative around a young woman's development. There were already thousands of such narratives, and readers loved them. The real difficulty was how to keep the reader sympathetic to a heroine *intentionally* endowed with the kind of instability that leads to grave self-betrayals. James addressed this problem with all his adroitness and in the process produced a work of fiction as long on beauty as it is short on moral candor.[19] In the end he produced a diminished picture of human freedom. Isabel's treacherous servility leads to a conservative sort of responsibility, which finds freedom only in the acceptance of traditional forms.

Reading *Daniel Deronda* several months before he first mentioned his own ambitious new novel, James was put off by the moralizing commentary − "the defects of later growth, of the author's style."[20] Constantius, the character closest to James in his sparkling "Daniel Deronda: A Conversation," feels that George Eliot's novel showed "a want of tact" in making "moral reflections" and setting forth "'views' upon life."[21] In both its moral reflections and its story content, James's novel was to be the antithesis of its discursive feminine forebears and rivals. Not just tactful, it was to be a deliberately *un*forthcoming narrative, one that carefully veils its "views."

2

But *The Portrait of a Lady* emerged from more than James's critical response to an Anglo-American tradition of women's fiction. James created the novel by fusing his reading with elements of his personal life − his close friendship with his remarkable cousin Minnie Temple, his tremendous respect for his father and his philosophy of marriage, and his own curious feeling of impotence.

Most commentators seem disposed to assume that Isabel more or less reproduces Minnie. In December 1880 James's friend Grace Norton, having read only the first two numbers of the serial, wondered whether Isabel was a portrait of the cousin. James's reply constitutes his one surviving comment on this question of the closeness of his representation:

> You are both right & wrong about Minny Temple. I had her in mind
> & there is in the heroine a considerable infusion of my impression of

her remarkable nature. But the thing is not a portrait. Poor Minny
was essentially *incomplete* & I have attempted to make my young
woman more rounded, more finished.

One might assume from this that Minnie was incomplete because
she died young, or was ill and confined, or was prevented from
traveling to Italy, or some such thing, and that in his novel James
imagined what her life might have been if allowed to go on in
altered circumstances. James may have meant this, but he also
meant something quite different and more grandiose, as his next
sentence hints. "In truth every one, in life, is incomplete, & it is the
mark of art that in reproducing them one feels the desire to fill
them out, to justify them, as it were."[22] This suggests that Minnie's
incompleteness had less to do with her personality or early death
than with a defect endemic to all humanity. By the same token,
James's desire to reproduce her, to fill her out, had nothing to do
with *his* peculiar nature and relationship with her. Instead, he
claimed to be enacting an impulse characteristic of artists in general – the impulse not so much to create an imaginary person as to
perfect, and thus "justify," an actual one. Yet even as James wrote
this shocking word, which would be perfectly in character for the
meddling scientist who seeks to perfect his wife in Hawthorne's
tale, "The Birthmark," James backed away from his haughty and
transcendent claim, adding the mitigating phrase "as it were."

If we compare James's heroine to what we can reconstruct of his
cousin, it becomes clear that he had cause to feel uneasy about his
highhanded art. Isabel embodies a drastic reinterpretation of Minnie's character from a definite point of view. Although no author,
no matter how realistic, has an obligation to reproduce his models
accurately, the alterations he chooses to make can be extremely
revealing about the nature of his imaginative work.

Minnie's "pet theory"[23] was that one should always hold out
for a chance at the best, no matter how remote, rather than settle
for second best. In Chapter 6 James describes Isabel's version of
this high integrity as one of her "many theories":

> The girl had a certain nobleness of imagination which rendered her
> a good many services and played her a great many tricks. She spent

half her time in thinking of beauty, and bravery, and magnanimity. . . . She had an infinite hope that she should never do anything wrong. . . . [S]he had seen very little of the evil of the world, but she had seen women who lied and who tried to hurt each other. Seeing such things had quickened her high spirit; it seemed right to scorn them. Of course the danger of a high spirit is the danger of inconsistency. . . . Isabel . . . flattered herself that such contradictions would never be observed in her own conduct.

This passage is heavily premonitory, looking forward to Isabel's long and painful effort to maintain a noble, impassive front after her marriage goes bad. But there is no evidence of any kind that Minnie got in trouble by applying her favorite theory, or that she ever had cause to modify or regret it. "I believe it more than ever, every day I live,"[24] she wrote six months before her death from tuberculosis at the age of twenty-four. Less than two months from the end, she was able to dismiss the fevered religious conversion induced in her by Henry Sr.'s denunciation of her "*pride & conceit.*"[25] When James endowed Isabel with an untested need always to think well of herself, he was effectively deflating his cousin's rigorous integrity. He was saying that this firm self-reliance was a schoolgirlish pose, that it could not possibly survive intact, and should not.

There is a very interesting difference between the real woman's known opinions and Isabel's "many theories." Minnie's characteristic mode of thought seems to have been practical and anti-theoretical. She resisted Henry Sr.'s indoctrination because it "didn't touch my case a bit — didn't give me the least comfort or practical help." Her tragic mentality, her refusal to accept any sort of "happy Rest this side of Eternity,"[26] was far removed from Isabel's "fixed determination to regard the world as a place of brightness, of free expansion, of irresistible action" (Chap. 6). James transformed a person who had a down-to-earth openness toward experience and a proven independence of thought into a character who tended to lose touch with her feelings, to dwell on a complicated self-image involving noble and picturesque attitudes.

As Alice Wellington Rollins pointed out in 1884, Isabel does not have "a particle of humor."[27] But Cousin Minnie had a teasing, bantering side that comes out in relief in her letters to the wooden John *Chip*man Gray, who was probably the chief model for Caspar Good*wood*. When she threatened to take up the study of law or invited Gray to disguise himself as a woman in order to accompany her on a trip, she was displaying the sort of humor that, like Penelope Lapham's, implicitly challenges propriety and the strict nineteenth-century separation of sexes. James excised these daring sallies from Minnie's letters as reproduced in *Notes of a Son*, motivated perhaps by the fear that unless she was censored she might seem vulgar. Isabel's humorlessness tells us much less about the so-called American girl of the period than about James's own nervous fastidiousness.

The easy, comradely tone of Minnie's letters to Gray marks a key difference in the two women's male friendships. Minnie was on close terms with several highly masculine men, William James and Oliver Wendell Holmes, Jr., among them. Although these friendships turned tense and involved at times, they were considerably less stiff and more reciprocal than Isabel's relationships with Goodwood and Lord Warburton, whose romantic pursuit (to some extent required by the novel-form itself) puts her on the defensive. In old age Gray looked back on his acquaintance with Minnie in these terms: "I . . . was never in love with her. 'I liked better to write to her than to see her.' She was the only *just* woman I have ever known. Her friendship is one of the things in my life which I best like to remember."[28] In "completing" Minnie, James retained that prickliness that caused Gray to prefer to communicate with her in letters rather than face to face. Similarly, young men are "afraid" of Isabel, believing "that some special preparation was required for talking with her" (Chap. 4). But James eliminated Minnie's capacity for dealing with forceful men on a basis of relaxed equality.

Surviving documents have nothing to say about Minnie's memories of and feelings for her father, who died in 1854, when she was eight. But she remembered her mother (who died later that year) with warm feelings, recalling in her teens that the face of a brother killed at Chancellorsville had a *"sweet heavenly* smile . . . which always made me think of heaven and Mama."[29] With Isabel, however, the mother isn't mentioned, the father being the parent who is fondly remembered.

When Minnie attended a young ladies' academy in 1862 and 1863, she shared a room with Helena de Kay,[30] and the two girls became extremely close friends. During vacations they engaged in an intense schoolgirl correspondence. Minnie's surviving letters are lavish in their expression of affection. "And now what is my own darling doing tonight?" begins one, and further on: "Good Night my Blessing. I will try and do without your dear, *motherly* care tonight, but it will be very hard." Another says, "I am afraid you need a little 'titeru' which I will also have in readiness for you upon your arrival."[31] Following a rebellion of some kind by the pupils during the spring 1863 term, Margaret Robertson, one of the two sisters in charge of the institution, sent letters to both Helena's mother and Henry James, Sr., with whom Minnie was to spend spring break. Mrs. de Kay promptly wrote her daughter, advising that Minnie's character was still unsettled and her influence should be resisted. The schoolmistress's letter to the Jameses was read by Minnie during her Newport visit. Judging by her report to Helena, this letter warned that the two girls were so close they did each other "a *great deal* of harm," encouraging each other to "forget . . . the rest of the human race." Minnie's blunt response: "Ha! ha! ha! — I don't agree with her."[32] Nineteen-year-old Henry James was at home then; a letter written decades later to Helena confirms that he was aware of "your young, your younger intimacy"[33] with Minnie. The relationship between Isabel Archer and *her* longtime best friend, Henrietta, lacks this intimate and juvenile character. Isabel seems to have lost much of her affection for her friend, being chiefly concerned to resist her intrusive advice and criticism. It is as if James has put into effect the teacher's wishes and separated Minnie from a bad feminine influence, thus weakening the sororal relationship along with the maternal and fraternal ones. In the end Isabel's closest bond is with her male cousin.

Divorce as a topic is strangely absent from Isabel's life and mind, yet shows up in an interesting way in Minnie's. In 1869 one of her friends, Ella Dietz Clymer, apparently attempted without success to get out of an unwise early marriage. Minnie alluded to this effort in a letter to her lawyer friend Gray: "By the way I don't know whether she has been divorced from that man or not. I have heard it contradicted."[34] Evidently, the option of divorce was respectable enough for Minnie that she felt comfortable discussing it with Gray (though not with Clymer herself). In Isabel's world, however, legal divorce seems to be unmentionable or inconceivable. Curiously, one of Henrietta's American friends traveling in Europe happens to be named *Climber*. There will be proposals of marriage, Henrietta warns Isabel: "Annie Climber was asked three times in Italy – poor plain little Annie" (Chap. 17). It is fascinating that James reached back to Minnie's circle for this name. The real Clymer was known for her beauty and was an active and prominent feminist. In 1868 she played a decisive role in organizing the most important early women's club in America, Sorosis, and at the time James wrote *The Portrait* she seems to have passed the peak of her acting career on the London stage.[35] Did James's respelling of her last name represent a snide judgment upon a prominent public woman who apparently refused (unlike Isabel) to accept a bad marriage?

Minnie's views on marriage were definitely advanced for her time. Even the well-seasoned Mary Chesnut had been scandalized in 1864 to learn that the author of *Adam Bede* was living with George Henry Lewes,[36] but five years later the unmarried Minnie not only took this awkward fact for granted but wondered in a letter (to Gray, not James) how George Eliot's "lofty moral sentiments have served her practically – for instance in her dealings with Lewes."[37] Also, she doubted whether others would enter matrimony if they felt as she did about the institution,[38] thus differing radically with her spiritual adviser, Uncle Henry, who made marriage a means of salvation. When her sister Kitty got engaged to a man over twenty years her senior, James's letter of congratulation slyly asked how Minnie "in that deep inscrutable soul of hers contemplates your promotion. It is a rare chance for Minny's cogitations – heaven bless her! If she could drop me a line I should be very glad to have her views."[39] This sounds as if he sniffed Minnie's disapproval. After a second sister, Elly, got engaged to a man almost thirty years her elder, James no longer had cause to feel uncertain about Minnie's judgment. "I must confess my imagination had taken higher flights in the way of a spouse for Elly," she wrote him, using an image he would later attribute to Ralph Touchett. As for her own future, she was categorical: "I have quite determined that the line must be drawn *here*." Unlike her sisters, she was resolved never to "become the prey of a bald-headed Emmet."[40]

Minnie could not have foreseen that she would become the prey of her slightly older cousin. She had vigorously resisted that cousin's father, who advised her to renounce, but the heroine based on her has a secret dream of servitude that confirms the father's opinion: women are made to serve. Whereas Minnie was skeptical about indissoluble bonds, Isabel refuses to leave the tyrannical husband who hates her. James "completed" Minnie by having the mature Isabel reject the real woman's free-spiritedness.

The single most telling alteration James performed on Minnie was to make her dream of and then marry a middle-aged husband. Osmond isn't bald (his "hair, still dense, but prematurely grizzled, had been cropped close" [Chap. 22]), but he is almost twice Isabel's age, as Kitty's and Elly's husbands were. As the central event of his most ambitious novel yet, James required the character modeled on his cousin to do the one thing she emphatically told him she would not. If one couples this use of her with James's repeated claim that Minnie was fortunate to die young, that life would have proved treacherous to someone so spirited, one can sense how *The Portrait* secretly questions her strength and judgment. The novel says that she and other women who affront traditional constraints are weaker and more foolish than they suppose and that in the end, like the free-thinking heroine of Anne Moncure Crane's *Opportunity,* they are bound to do something "utterly pedantic and unnatural and insupportable."[41] James's scheme for "justifying" Minnie reveals a deeply rooted insistence on her folly.

The closer one looks at James's transformations of Minnie, the more one wonders if he was justifying, not her, but a mysterious and powerful drive to take over her life. The remarkably uninhibited letters he wrote his mother and older brother after learning of Minnie's death bespeak some such desire. "The more I think of her the more perfectly satisfied I am to have her translated from this changing realm of fact to the steady realm of thought. There she may bloom into a beauty more radiant than our dull eyes will avail to contemplate." "Translated" – it's as if Minnie had become some kind of text. "She was at any rate the helpless victim & toy of her own intelligence – so that there is positive relief in thinking of her being removed from her own heroic treatment & placed in kinder hands."[42] In this eerie sentence Minnie is remembered not as a creature, a being in nature who has died, but as the author of herself – writer and heroine together. Her mistake, that of the too-ambitious young artist, was to dream of too heroic a treatment of herself. Now, happily, the uncompleted manuscript has been transferred to a more indulgent writer, who will allow Minnie the gentle feminine development she spurned.

James's desire to take possession of Minnie and remake her was so strong and tenacious it would seem to be a founding motive in both his life and his art. In 1913, when he excerpted her 1869–70 correspondence for *Notes of a Son,* he fraudulently ascribed to her a passage composed by himself:

> This climate [in New York] is trying, to be sure, but such as it is I've got to take my chance in it, as there is *no one I care enough for,* or who cares enough for me, *to take charge of me* to Italy, or to the south anywhere. I don't believe any climate, however good, would be of the least use to me with *people I don't care for.*[43]

With this fabrication James drastically compromised Minnie's independence of character and the closeness of her relations with her sister Kitty, with whom she had been living in 1869. The arrogance of this alteration of fact is shocking: not only would Minnie's survivors have been pained by the claim, twice repeated, that she didn't "care for" her people, but James's highhanded destruction of the letters effectively prevented anyone from clearing up the bad feelings. (The only reason we can detect the fraud is that William James's widow and daughter meticulously copied Minnie's letters before sending the originals on to James.)

What is particularly disturbing is that the transformations we can observe in this fraudulent passage are virtually the same as the alterations James performed on Minnie in order to create *The Portrait*. James built the novel precisely by pretending that Minnie was far less capable of taking care of herself, and far more alienated from friends and family, than she in fact was. He "took charge" of her, transformed her into a witness against her own will and history, and then said he was only completing and justifying her.

Yet James kept faith with Minnie by reproducing her stern sense of justice. Gray (who became an authority on property law) remembered her as "the only *just* woman" he had ever known. No reader of *The Portrait* has been more attentive to Isabel's passion for dealing justly with others than has Joseph Wiesenfarth, who shows how she resolves competing claims during her married years.[44] Wiesenfarth gives a fine exposition of her tough honorableness, yet leaves out something that seems crucial − Minnie's awareness of what would "touch my case," what was owing to herself. In creating this heroine, James required Minnie's passion for being just to others to crush her other more anarchic, freedom-loving impulses. He justified his cousin by demonstrating how a determination to be noble and just would in time refine away the crudity − and with it the independence.

If one tries to determine what James's immediate family and more distant relatives thought about his use of this remarkable cousin, one is in for a surprise. Even though James's letters home had billed the novel as his biggest and best yet, stimulating William to inquire as early as 1878 about the "great novel,"[45] there is not one surviving letter from any family member expressing an opinion about *The Portrait*. I can find only two faint hints. James's January 30, 1881, letter to his father informs us that Henry Sr. was critical of the Isabel−Henrietta friendship: "Thank you for your little criticism on the 'Portrait.' Yes, it appears unnatural, certainly, that Isabel should fraternize with Henrietta, but it wouldn't if I explained it."[46] (Henry Sr.'s reaction is reminiscent of the teacher's disapproval of Minnie and Helena's friendship.) Then there is a tantalizingly incomplete report in a letter Alice H. James sent William soon after *The Portrait*'s appearance as a book:

The night [Josiah] Royce called he talked delightfully of novels, very much disgusted with Howells's definition of the future novelist. He said some admirable things of Harry – the best *hostile* criticism I ever heard of him and when through he concluded with, "I don't know what Prof. James thinks of his brother's writings, but I should judge his opinion would be much like mine."[47]

Equally suggestive is the unexplained and never patched-up quarrel between Henry James and Minnie's sister Elly, who resented his appropriation of Minnie's letters in *Notes of a Son* and whose surrounding "depths of illiteracy"[48] he in return haughtily denounced. If we try to read James through Elly's eyes – Elly who briefly moved to California in 1869 with her elderly bridegroom – we can't help lingering over James's supercilious account of Isabel's sisters, particularly Edith, who unwillingly spends her life in "various military stations, chiefly in the unfashionable West" (Chap. 4). I predict that if Elly's letters of 1881–82 ever turn up, they will be found to be highly critical of James's use of her sister in creating *The Portrait*.

3

What should James's betrayal of Minnie Temple mean to us as readers and interpreters of *The Portrait of a Lady?* To answer this question, we must strive to plumb the soul of the heroine's possessive cousin. I mean not only Minnie's cousin Henry but Isabel's cousin Ralph, the spectator and secret arranger of her life. This strange man, who bears a special, nonerotic love for her and slowly dies from a lingering illness during the four years the novel covers, surely reflects in some devious way the author's own private state.[49] Just as surely, the differences between James and Ralph illuminate James's own appropriation of Minnie.

The chapter in which Isabel's engagement is made public also contains the first announcement of "the now apparently complete loss" of Ralph's health. Isabel sees that "he was dying" (Chap. 33), and the blunt phrase wipes out the studied ambiguity that has up to this point veiled his fate. This is a big revelation – but strange to say, both James and Isabel appear to forget it. Only five chapters later, after Ralph arrives in Rome, the following exchange takes place between Lord Warburton and Isabel:

> "I sometimes think he is dying," Lord Warburton said.
> Isabel started up.
> "I will go to him now!" (Chap. 38)

This curious and ineffective repetition identifies one of the novel's most Victorian features, Ralph's prolonged death, which is characterized less by the realistic treatment of tuberculosis than by the solemn drapery of significance. Each announcement that Ralph is dying follows upon a fresh sign of Isabel's tragic capitulation. The linkage is this: as the heroine goes down, the observant male cousin who lives through her suffers mortally. His slow decline conveys the ponderous sense of the operations of Nemesis that we get in other Victorian novels, in Crane's *Emily Chester* in particular, but the decline also tells us something about James himself.

Three decades after writing *The Portrait,* James admitted that in composing his second novel based on Minnie's image, *The Wings of the Dove,* he had felt uneasy about the "idea of making one's protagonist 'sick'." He decided he could avoid the taint of morbid interest by imputing to the dying heroine "the unsurpassable activity of passionate, of inspired resistance." A writer, he wisely argued, "essentially *can't* be concerned with the act of dying. Let him deal with the sickest of the sick, it is still by the act of living that they appeal to him." This said, James recollected his various "accessory invalids," naming Ralph Touchett but only to insist that he was an anomaly. Rather than contributing a sense of morbidity, he was "a positive good mark, a direct aid to pleasantness and vividness." James could not explain why sick Ralph wasn't morbid when sick Millie so easily could have been, but he emphatically denied that the difference had anything to do with "his fact of sex."[50]

In fact, Ralph is a version of a sickly and specifically male type that was so important for James he could not detect its morbidity. The type appears in two of his earliest short stories in which a badly wounded Civil War veteran, hanging between life and death, dies after discovering that the young woman he thought

71

was pledged to him has accepted another man's proposal. In "The Story of a Year" (1865), published when James was only twenty-one, John Ford, brave and generous, persuades Lizzie Crowe to keep their engagement secret as he goes off to battle, in this way leaving her free. Unfortunately, the noble man doesn't suspect that Lizzie, as James tells us with surprising directness, is a "poor misinformed creature."[51] She soon falls in love with a second handsome man and accepts his proposal. When John, now gravely injured, learns of the vain and easily swayed girl's faithlessness, he goes into a rapid decline and dies. In the second story, "A Most Extraordinary Case" (1868), the protagonist is once again a desperately unwell young man who has had little experience of women's ways. Ferdinand Mason is not engaged to Caroline Hofmann but he feels that they share an unspoken compact: he has "extracted from her words a delicate assurance that he could afford to wait"[52] before eventually proposing. Caroline, however, is put before us as a hard and self-sufficing woman, one who lacks the refined consideration the officer imputes to her. In the end the news that she has gotten engaged to someone else destroys Ferdinand's will to live, and he too suffers a relapse and dies. In each of these sickly narratives an unwell man feels let down by a woman who proves to be less affectionate, refined, and trustworthy than he had counted on. The stories are stiffly accusatory, not of the man who fails to act out a passionate and inspired resistance, but of the woman who disappoints him.

These early and unsuccessful stories are important because they introduce the material James would rework in *The Portrait*, in which Ralph is seen to be "dying" the moment Isabel's engagement becomes known. As Leon Edel has pointed out, Isabel is a complicated, more sympathetic version of James's early killer-Dianas. After turning down Lord Warburton, Isabel wonders, with reason, "whether she were not a cold, hard girl" (Chap. 12). She lets Caspar Goodwood understand that if he should hear of her engagement, he may "venture to doubt it" (Chap. 16), and he does. She gives him permission to try her again in two years, and he does this too. Warburton isn't an officer, but he is associated with the Dying Gladiator when Isabel dismisses him in Chapter 28.

In her dealings with Ralph, Warburton, and Goodwood, Isabel makes the same moves as James's early hard, heartless heroines. Behind James's critical treatment of her stand these early resentful narratives, and behind Ralph lie John Ford and Ferdinand Mason. What James did over a period of fifteen years with these two dying characters was to peel away the factitious elements and embody them in accessory figures. The jilted-suitor aspect became Goodwood; the dying-soldier aspect turned into Warburton, the Dying Gladiator. What remained was the sickly spectatorial dependency on a heroine, and this, the heart of the matter, evolved into Ralph. If Isabel's manly suitors often seem rather wooden and unfelt, that is partly because their segments of the original material were outside the orbit of James's knowledge, interests, and experience. The only part that was inside was what went into the richly imagined Ralph.

Sickly dependency on an observed heroine with a stirring life of her own: this material, closely related to James's identity problems as an adolescent and to the women's novels he was reading, generated Ralph and Isabel. The first volume of Leon Edel's biography interprets this material in a way I believe to be partly mistaken. According to Edel, the dying-officer stories inform us that James adored Minnie in a distant, even humiliated, way and that this worship reflected a more general view that women were dangerous and unfathomable Dianas:

> Henry in reality wanted only to worship Minny from a quiet and discreet – and we might add safe – distance. . . . To sit back and observe his cousin, to worship her from afar, to give her signs of devotion at the real right moment, this seems to have been the love stratagem of Henry – as it was of a number of his early young fictional heroes. . . . *True love is best by silence known.* And such silence can have in it a component of fear. . . . Henry James feared women and worshipped them and hesitated to express his feelings lest he be turned away.[53]

Much of this seems dubious – the claim that James's attitudes toward Minnie were representative of his attitudes toward women in general; the assumption that his early fictional heroes tell us in some transparent way about his own real-life feelings; the omission of all reference to contemporary thought and fiction about women. I know of no firm biographical evidence that James was fearful of women, although his memoirs show plainly that he was intimidated by the taunts, tricks, and superior capacities of boys and men. Above all, what does it mean to say that James "loved" Minnie, especially since he himself denied the imputation in a letter home? Any sound interpretation of his feelings for and appropriation of Minnie must somehow take into account the homoeroticism that erupted in him in the 1890s, a subject rightly emphasized in Edel's later volumes.

In ,order to thread one's way through the difficulties (and the gaps in the record), we need to distinguish between James's direct and spontaneous feelings for Minnie and his representation of these feelings when absent from her – especially when writing about her to William or for other male readers. On the first point, the evidence suggests that even though he was almost three years older than Minnie, he was so close and affectionate he could almost be called kittenish. One of Minnie's early letters, to which Edel was not given access, offers this revealing glimpse of Henry and William in 1863: "Willy James is the same strange youth as ever, stranger if possible, but good as ever. He is not *cross* to me, but I think he has rather *renounced* me, in the depths of his heart, as a *bad* thing. Harry is as *lovely* as ever, verily the *goodness* of that boy passeth human comprehension."[54] One would suppose that if anyone chose to debunk Minnie "as a *bad* thing" it would have been Willy, not Harry, who, here and in other letters, looks from her perspective like a sweet, affectionate, and unfathomable comrade. But even though her slightly patronizing report, written in the present tense from the James's parlor in Newport, would seem to make cousin Harry's betrayal of her more mystifying than ever, the passage provides the crucial information that is needed to solve the mystery.

The fact is, *William* disliked Minnie, at least as early as 1863 and as late as the winter of 1868–69, and he was not the only one. James's father, mother, and sister also felt a persistent hostility toward her. Minnie's letter of 1863 was written from enemy territory, so to speak. Henry Jr. was the only member of his family who felt and showed any real sweetness for her. The fundamental reason he betrayed his defiantly independent cousin was to reaffirm his loyalty to the strongly patriarchal values of his family, particularly as expressed by his father and older brother.

There is room here for only the briefest sketch of James's complicated situation. One reason for his closeness to his orphaned cousin was that she fulfilled his early and tremendously important orphan fantasy, in which he and his brothers and sister were "sent separately off among cold or even cruel aliens in order to be there thrillingly homesick."[55] Another reason is that he lived on extremely uneasy terms with the aggressive male world of his time. Deeply "feminine," James projected himself onto his strong cousin, as onto certain heroines of fiction, but simultaneously remained in thrall to William and Henry James, Sr., two extremely vigorous and forceful men who not only insisted on reactionary views of female emancipation but specifically disapproved of Minnie's self-assertiveness. The father was a nineteenth-century seer on the woman question, arguing over and over that marriage was a sacrament in which woman devoted herself to the redemption of man. In 1870 Henry Jr. let his family know three times that he agreed with Henry Sr.'s views, as if it was crucial to stand with the family on this matter.[56] James was divided between a warm attachment to Minnie and the necessity (extremely pressing during the Civil War) of proving himself to be a man. It was because of his determined loyalty to the world of men that he represented his early dying soldiers (and later Ralph) as in terrible jeopardy from heartless Dianas. James *had* to betray Minnie and his own affection; the only way to win respect in the world of the fathers was to take captive the Amazon who had challenged them. James "completed" Minnie in order to make her – *and himself* – acceptable to the patriarchy.

My point is that James's career as a fiction writer began, not with any sort of direct transcription of his experience, but with just the opposite – a remarkably polished effort to put his own experience totally out of the question.[57] The early fiction sets in operation a severe and dignified program of transformation. That is one reason why the early dying-soldier stories have such a conspicuous conservative rhetoric. Writing in clear opposition to the current trends in women's fiction, James wanted to demonstrate that things would unravel if women renounced their sacred pledges. Both "The Story of a Year" and "A Most Extraordinary Case" declare that the modern American woman's abandonment of her redemptive mission – her refusal to be affectionate, faithful, refined – will destroy the man who trusts her, especially if he is a traditional man still loyal to the claims of honor in war and in polite society.

Going to particulars, "The Story of a Year" strongly reacts to Rebecca Harding Davis's *Atlantic Monthly* serial of 1861–62, "A Story of To-Day," whose title James probably adapted, and Crane's *Emily Chester* (1864). In the former narrative the heroine abandons her philanthropic devotion in favor of romantic love; in the latter she develops an irresistible physical repugnance for her husband and a strange "supersensuous" attraction to another man. Each work treats the heroine's change of heart with notable sympathy, and James's story indirectly rebukes both. In reviewing *Emily Chester* he expressed the same outrage at the title character's psychological infidelity that his own story shows for Lizzie Crowe's fickleness. The review denounced Emily's helpless preference for another man over her husband, and strenuously argued that morality, not magnetic psychology, was what fiction must attend to. James went so far as to call the book immoral because it failed to say that the heroine had an obligation to "conquer a peace." Any wife, in fiction or out, "who indulges in a foolish passion, without even the excuse of loving well, must be curtly and sternly dismissed."[58] In line with such preachments, James led the reader of his own story to dismiss Lizzie Crowe as curtly and sternly as possible: her vacant-mindedness must not be tolerated. In the scene where she forgets her wounded fiancé and allows her fancy to run after handsome Mr. Bruce, the narrator magisterially assures us that her "intellect was unequal to the stern logic of human events."[59]

"The Story of a Year" was published in March 1865 in the *Atlantic*. A letter from James to Thomas Sergeant Perry implies that the narrative had been written by the previous March, seven

76

months before the publication of *Emily Chester*. But there is reason to believe James revised and shortened his story in November 1864, at the same time he confronted Crane's novel. He had originally called his work a "modern novel" and a "novelette," categories that suggest it would not have fit into a single issue of the *Atlantic*. Furthermore, his October 28, 1864, letter commenting on the magazine's notice of acceptance grumbles, in an ambiguous phrase, that "it is so little."[60] The mysterious phrase probably refers, not to the size of James's payment, as has been suggested, but to the *Atlantic*'s length requirements. James T. Fields, the editor, regularly tried to squeeze short fiction into a single issue.

The likelihood that James was asked to shorten his first signed narrative is all the more significant because of the coincidental dates. On October 15 James had written Charles Eliot Norton proposing to review *Emily Chester*, but the letter was unaccountably held up: a memorandum in Norton's meticulous hand on the back of the sheet reads, "Recd. Octr 29th. Ansd. 30th."[61] James, meanwhile, was waiting for the reply. His October 28 letter to Perry reveals that he had not yet begun reading the book. Thus, events conspired so that he read and reviewed *Emily Chester* at the same time he took his own "modern novel" in hand for condensation. James's first American narrative, then, probably reflects his hostile response to a recent novel dealing with a woman's magnetic disorders. His career as a fiction writer may have begun in a literal attempt to chasten and correct a currently influential account, by a woman, of women's experience. And just as James's review showed strong sympathy for Emily's husband, so the story resentfully declared that it is not the faithless woman who will die, as in Crane's novel, but the abandoned man.

The second story, "A Most Extraordinary Case," constitutes a connecting link between "The Story of a Year" and *The Portrait*. Caroline Hofmann, the heroine, is more ambiguous than Lizzie, so that it is hard to know whether she or her idealizing admirer is more at fault. For much of the story she almost appears to be James's second portrait of a noble, civilized lady (the first being Adela Moore of "A Day of Days").[62] We can't help wondering whether the dying man's conviction that he and Caroline share a delicate pact is a delusion. But then comes the scene where Caroline descends to the Hudson River and sings German lieder, simultaneously imitating the Lorelei, who lured mariners to their death, and wearying Ferdinand to the point of exhaustion. At the party, where she and some other American girls further wear out the hero, it appears that Caroline actively contributes to his death. A bystander points the moral: "Was there ever anything like the avidity of these dreadful girls?"[63] In the original version one of the lethal defeminized girls was named Miss McCarthy, but when James reworked the narrative in 1884–85 for *Stories Revived*, he renamed her Miss Masters, a change that underscores her dominating masculinity. But the Diana-like heroine is less blatant.

James's impulse to punish women's restless heroines was becoming less obtrusive. At times his outrage would moderate into a project of rehabilitation: *The Portrait* shows how a rather thoughtless girl turns into a noble lady precisely by enduring the miserable marriage that Crane's and Alcott's heroines couldn't stand. The uncanny thing is that James announced this general project in the text of "A Most Extraordinary Case." The doctor says of Caroline Hofmann: "She looks as if she had come out of an American novel. I don't know that that's great praise; but, at all events, I make her come out of it." Ferdinand's prescient response: "You're bound in honour, then . . . to put her into another."[64]

James entered the craft of fiction as a severe and precocious professional whose narratives bore a critical relation to existing literary modes and tastes. He was impregnated with some very idealistic notions of propriety and morality: some things were sacred. He was correspondingly alienated, and would remain so until his fifties, from much of his own experience, and thus his fiction was devoted to noble ideas that, taken as a point of observation and judgment, made life look rather cheap. One of the fundamental impulses in his fiction was not to reproduce or reflect life but to neutralize, devulgarize, dignify it — "justify" it. The disjunction between his art and his life baffles any naive project of recovering that life from his fictional narratives. It's not that the life isn't there, in every finely turned phrase, but that it's so meticulously and thoroughly worked up, like timber transformed into inlaid veneer.

And so we return again to *The Portrait,* to see where its beautifully finished and varnished surface reveals the original twisted grain. The place to look is in James's two portraits of gentlemen, Ralph Touchett and Gilbert Osmond.

4

The great paradox in James's imaginative development is that he broke through to his most important material by inventing people whose lives are empty. Ralph is set before us so richly and beautifully because he captures so much of his creator's distance from life. Many readers feel that Ralph's generosity, truthfulness, tolerance, and lack of dogmatism reflect James's own best qualities. Yet it's obvious that Ralph isn't a simple self-portrait. His shabby attire, vagrant humor, idleness, and stalled career suffice to rule out any straightforward equivalence. More important, Ralph's hopes for Isabel are far more naive than are those of the author, who sees Isabel as folly-ridden. The key difference is that, where James believed Minnie was fortunately prevented by her death from wading into some tragic downfall, Ralph acts to increase Isabel's power of self-expression. In doing so, he is animated by a particular mental image: "I had a sort of vision of your future. . . . I amused myself with planning out a kind of destiny for you. . . . You seemed to me to be soaring far up in the blue – to be sailing in the bright light, over the heads of men" (Chap. 34). Ralph's private daydream is based on light and shadow, like Isabel's favorite picture of the refined father and his still daughter. But where Ralph likes to think of Isabel aloft and in brightness, she herself prefers "the atmosphere of summer twilight" (Chap. 26). Tragically, Ralph founds his life on *his* pictured daydream, just as Isabel relies on her own, and when she inevitably disappoints his dream he declares, "it hurts me . . . as if I had fallen myself!" (Chap. 34)

Readers coming fresh to James might sensibly conclude that Ralph's error is to try to live someone else's life rather than his own. But James was not the kind of man to dramatize such plain truths. He himself lived in the "constant hum of borrowed experience,"[65] and Ralph's sunlit vision of Isabel recapitulates the very imagery James was fond of in his twenties. In 1867 he had loved Crane's heroine in *Opportunity* for being "a strong and free young girl" who "has her face to the sun." He had criticized Alcott because she let the heroine of *Moods* succumb to "the shadow."[66] His own first novel, written a few years later, told of a heroine whose fancy was temporarily darkened by the "cooling shadow" of unworthy suitors but who finally emerged into airy light: "the sky was blazing blue overhead; the opposite side of the street was all in sun; she hailed the joyous brightness of the day with a kind of answering joy."[67] Nine years later, writing *The Portrait,* James assigned light and dark the same basic values – but without the optimism. Isabel meets her eventual master in a cool, poorly windowed apartment, is treacherously stirred by Osmond's attractive picture of a life conducted in "the shadows just lengthening" (Chap. 35), and then slowly realizes that she has been led into "the house of darkness, the house of dumbness, the house of suffocation" (Chap. 42). Pansy is already a flower of the shade. Following Osmond's orders, she waits for the shadow to reach a certain line before stepping into the bright sunlit garden (Chap. 30).

It would seem, then, that Ralph embodies a vital phase of the author's own developing imagination. The passionate cultivation of a glowing picture of Isabel reproduces James's own early quest for a female champion. But there is this difference: Ralph is impaired, only half a man. He lacks his maker's deep suspicion of female independence, suspicion that counteracted James's identification with female heroism and bright Minnie Temple and thus saved him from being Ralph Touchett. Behind this suspicion stood Henry Sr.'s conservative doctrine on sexual difference – a doctrine Henry Jr. endorsed three times the year Minnie died.

The key fact about Ralph is that Isabel is only his second passion, the first being his father, Daniel Touchett. "Such slender faculty of reverence as he [Ralph] possessed," James announces, "centred wholly upon his father" (Chap. 7). The son admires Mr. Touchett as "a man of genius" and "enjoy[s] . . . the opportunity of observing him" (Chap. 5). Father and son are "close companions," so much so that the latter has long hoped and taken "for granted" that he will be the first to die. If Ralph is "steeped in melancholy" when Isabel enters his life, his outlook lying "under the shadow of a deeper cloud" (Chap. 7), it's not because of his invalidism. He is depressed because his father's illness took a fatal turn for the worse the preceding spring. The loving son dreads the inevitable separation.

This passionate filial attachment merits our closest scrutiny. Although James was not one to represent ideally positive characters, Daniel Touchett comes very close to being the perfect father. He combines a penetrating shrewdness with an amiable and reassuring mildness, in this way exhibiting Adam Verver's union of power and love in *The Golden Bowl*. Daniel's "genial acuteness" (Chap. 8) − elsewhere "veiled acuteness" − is such that he anticipates Warburton's misadventure with Isabel and Isabel's own susceptibility to "the fortune-hunters" (Chap. 18). He has acquired a fortune in banking, a beautiful English country house, and what would appear to be (within the novel) some sharp insights into class and character in England. His skepticism about upper-class "radicalism" (a term so vague one cannot say what issues are involved) is clearly intended to be seen as shrewd. As for his own political sympathies, Daniel is fundamentally conservative, amused by the way people take up "progressive ideas" and indifferent to proposed reforms so long as he can retain his accumulations: "You see they want to disestablish everything; but I'm a pretty big landowner here, and I don't want to be disestablished" (Chap. 8). All this, yet Daniel remains the epitome of kindness and pleasant blandness, a man of self-made wealth and power who seems to have been declawed. James even claims that his "feeling about his own position in the world was quite of the democratic sort" (Chap. 5).

Not only is Daniel Touchett a godlike Daddy Warbucks fantasy figure, but Ralph's devotion also seems too good to be true. Would a son who has "no great fancy" (Chap. 5) for the bank his father runs, who takes no more interest in it "than in the state of Patagonia" (Chap. 34), love to study the old man's mental operations? Ralph's conspicuous neglect of Mr. Touchett's great achievement does not seem consistent with James's insistence on the closeness of their bond. During his eighteen months in a subordinate position at the bank, Ralph was fonder of "walking about" than working at his "high stool" (Chap. 5); it was while so employed that he first showed symptoms of his fatal disease. After his father's death, he not only lets the firm drift into some kind of trouble but ignores his mother's advice "to see what they were doing at the bank" (Chap. 39). Exhibiting no uneasiness at all over this unconvincing father-and-son business, James innocently asks us to believe that the son lives chiefly to nurse his aged father and cherishes a secret dream of dying with him.

Ralph's filial attachment is one of those segments of Jamesian narrative in which an extremely correct and depleted version of human behavior gets substituted for the real and living thing. It's like what James saw in *Emily Chester,* theory masquerading as feeling – except that James is tame where Crane is wild.

Most curious of all, for a novel absolutely devoid of happy family life, Ralph's filial attachment is one of *three* intense father-child bonds. In handling Isabel's and Pansy's worship of *their* fathers, James wants us to see through the daughter's devotion. With Ralph, however, the authorial detachment appears to collapse.

What we are dealing with here is James's unconscious projection onto Ralph, with James exposing more than he intended of the obligatory or slavish aspect of his relationship with his father. Mr. Touchett's bank corresponds to Henry Sr.'s philosophy, which Henry Jr. for the most part avoided even while continuing to regard his father as a great not-to-be-questioned thinker, especially on "woman" and marriage. Given such attitudes, it makes sense that James was unable to detect the hollowness of Ralph's primal passion. It also makes sense that James exhibited this passion as a rival of Ralph's great spectatorial interest in his lively American cousin. Ralph's turn from his dying father to his cousin effectively translates the dialectic of James's own mind, caught between an allegiance to the paternal doctrine on women and marriage and a private absorption in untamed heroines.

The centrality of this opposition explains why Ralph takes such a dreadful risk in delivering his father's money to Isabel, and why the revelations of Isabel's mistake repeatedly get yoked to Ralph's "dying." Mr. Touchett held the money. Isabel has been given his substance. She grows rich the instant the banker-father dies. Her empowerment, that is to say, derives from his extinction, and this vital transfer has been engineered by none other than the supposedly loyal son. This is the reason Ralph must die: he has recklessly handed over the patriarch's vital stuff to a girl who can't help squandering it, and the fathers are not to be appeased.

Ralph is the scapegoat, made to pay the supreme price for exercising the author's suppressed impulse toward freedom and hope. Hence Ralph's best intentions only serve to usher Isabel into the old father-daughter marriage after all. Pansy resists such a marriage (to Warburton) and gets punished. Ralph, intending to free Isabel once and for all, inadvertently sells her into slavery and is punished even more. One of the novel's grimmest moments comes when Ralph realizes that his desperate final strategy for drawing Isabel out of Osmond's reach is to be successful only in the short term. She tells Ralph she doesn't "think anything is over" between her husband and herself. "'Are you going back to him?' Ralph stammered" (Chap. 54). Her return demonstrates that she believes in Ralph's ideal of freedom less than in her husband's defense of the indissoluble bond: "I take our marriage seriously. . . . I am not aware that we are divorced or separated; for me we are indissolubly united. You are nearer to me than any human creature, and I am nearer to you. . . . I think we should accept the consequences of our actions" (Chap. 51). Whether spoken sincerely or not, this speech expresses the position the novel works out. If Isabel is to make the right choice at the end, to follow the "very straight path" (Chap. 55) and thus become the "consistently wise" (Chap. 12) woman James actually steps in to tell us she will be, she must oppose Ralph's plan and return to her husband.

The whole opposition between Ralph and Osmond is one of the richest and best worked out elements in *The Portrait*. Their antagonistic relationship is presented with far more mastery than Ralph's unconvincing bond with his father. Ralph could not care less about establishing an identity before others, but Osmond, who depends on the illusionist's art for his place in the world, cares about little else. While Ralph has Harvard, Oxford, a big banking house, and an early Tudor mansion to back him up, Osmond takes his derivation from an affected mother who wished to be known as the American Corinne. Ralph has so much tradition he's bored by it, but Osmond, having nothing, turns into a complete snob, an emperor without a country. The former is the son of a self-made financier and landed proprietor, while the latter is a tyrant who enshrines himself in bric-a-brac and old medals, talks of being the Pope of Rome, and exhibits a perfect daughter and wife to the public. Osmond detests Ralph: "But that long jackanapes, the son — is he about the place?" (Chap. 22) This contemptuous and antiquated word (James's only other use of it, as far as I know, is in connection with the "crazy" Costa Rican envoy in *Roderick Hudson*)[68] catches Osmond's feeling that Ralph is too foolish, shapeless, and witless to stake out a dignified position in society. Osmond is wrong about Ralph, but Ralph, who in this connection as in others does enjoy an aristocratic advantage over Osmond, easily sees through the "sterile dilettante" (Chap. 34). Ralph's insight into Osmond's act is so lucid and unmediated that he can't imagine Isabel's inability to detect the sham. He even knows "by instinct, in advance" (Chap. 45) how Osmond will punish Isabel for Warburton's withdrawal.

Judging by the written comment on *The Portrait,* it would seem that no reader has ever doubted the truth of Ralph's insight into Osmond (certainly I do not). But there is a remarkable anomaly in the whole rich antagonism between the two men: it lacks all semblance of a *narrative* basis. Each character is *already* equipped with a complete opinion of the other, and one of them, Ralph, evidently sees through the other with the author's eyes. The text, however, brings the two characters together only once, at St. Peter's, where Ralph gets a shock on seeing Osmond with Isabel:

> On perceiving the gentleman from Florence, Ralph Touchett exhibited symptoms of surprise which might not perhaps have seemed flattering to Mr. Osmond. It must be added, however, that these manifestations were momentary, and Ralph was presently able to say to his cousin, with due jocularity, that she would soon have all her friends about her. His greeting to Mr. Osmond was apparently

frank; that is, the two men shook hands and looked at each other.
(Chap. 27)

James's manner here is so bland that he scarcely indicates the
settled enmity. In revision, he did two interesting things with the
passage. He made the irony heavier, so that instead of merely
showing surprise Ralph now appears "to take the case as not
committing him to joy."[69] And James deleted the last sentence,
thus doing away with the solitary contact between the two chief
male architects of Isabel's fate. In combination with the many
other revisions that stress Ralph's fear and hatred of Osmond (see,
for example, the Ralph—Warburton conversation that ends volume
1), the New York Edition thus enhances the paradoxical situation
of the first edition: an implacable opposition between two characters who never collide.

Is it a lapse that two central and mutually antagonistic characters should fail to meet in a novel as well plotted and as dramatic
as *The Portrait?* Perhaps not, though it is certainly a striking omission and one that invites comment. The tension of Isabel's life
would not be dissipated, nor the story materially altered, if James
had allowed Ralph and Osmond at least to cross swords. *The Portrait* is not like *The Ambassadors,* where Madame de Vionnet and
Mrs. Newsome *must* deal with one another chiefly through Strether and other envoys, or else the novel won't work. Osmond's
scenes with Warburton and Goodwood are extremely effective.
Why can't he have a scene with Ralph?

The answer, I believe, goes back to Ralph's improbable primal
passion for his father and to Henry Jr.'s loyalty to Henry Sr. Faithful
Ralph must not face Osmond because Osmond represents the dark
side of his, and his author's, male parent. They, along with the late
Mr. Archer, share a number of characteristics with each other —
and with Henry James, Sr. They are all divorced from American
life, have no niche in society, and are adulated by their children.
Although the novel strongly insists on the difference between Mr.
Touchett and Osmond, this difference almost vanishes if we try the
experiment of regarding the two parents from the point of view of
their fond children. Doing so, we see that the two children have a

similar filial bond. Ralph idolizes the acuity of his father's "genius," which is never authenticated for us, just as Pansy feels that Osmond "knows everything" (Chap. 37). Both children love to study their fathers and to gratify them. Both are in theory grown up, yet their maturity is ambiguous and we see them chiefly at home fondly tending the parent. Osmond's mocking question as to whether the jackanapes – followed by "the son" in apposition – is still "about the place" focuses exactly on this grotesque immaturity. We know Ralph by his first name, as sons and heroines are known, but Osmond goes by his last like other men. Just as James exaggerates Ralph's closeness to Mr. Touchett, he exaggerates the separation from Osmond, and the reason is simple: Ralph must not learn the truth about his father. But it is precisely because Osmond *is* the father that Ralph already knows him so mysteriously well.

Of course the novel insists that the Daniel–Ralph relationship is loving and the Gilbert–Pansy one cruel and vicious. But we may safely question Henry Jr.'s authority in making this distinction. He too worshipped his father-philosopher and found it difficult to tell the difference between paternal love and authoritarianism. Even while he remorselessly exposed the emptiness, isolation, cruel will, and magic arts behind Osmond's quiet parental facade, James showed no awareness that Ralph's own filial adoration is suspect. Even while emphasizing Pansy's subjection, the filial author did not question Ralph's fondness for tending his empire-building father and his dream of dying with him. If we ask what kind of novelist could possibly ask us to accept this idyllic father-son bond, the answer is irresistible. He must have been a Pansy.

James sensed that behind the benign mask the philosopher of marriage was a male Medusa. The only way a faithful son could gaze at that face was through fiction – the magical reflecting surface that turns a familiar object into something safely alien. The face that flashed in the mirror was Osmond's. The creative power that fused *The Portrait* came, precisely, from James's effort to confront, in the mirror, his father's authoritarianism – the authoritarianism that had sent Alice to spend a winter with an antifeminist physician specializing in women's troubles, just as Osmond sends Pansy back

86

to the convent. At one and the same time Osmond is the great evil presence and the spokesman for the most solemn and ultimate truths. He and Isabel *are* "indissolubly united." She *does* have too many ideas ("theories" is the author's word), and she grows conspicuously more elegant, thoughtful, honest, and responsible by entering and then choosing to reenter the house of bondage.

Predicated on Henry Sr.'s dogmas about women and marriage, *The Portrait* is the artifact of a brilliant but uneasy pansy. The conclusion, structured in such a way as to show Isabel rejecting passionate love and reaffirming her marriage vows, endorses Henry Sr.'s much repeated revelation: "love is a great reality to experience, but is so little an *end* of human life, that I have no regard for it save as ministering to marriage."[70] Separation or divorce might make sense to practical Henrietta, but Isabel belongs to a higher order and thus swears allegiance to the sacred bondage that constituted Henry Sr.'s essential message to the world:

> The law is . . . just, and even good, though it slay me. Yes, death at its hands were better than life at the risk of its dishonor at my hands. So I abide by my marriage bond. I see very well that the bond ought to be loosened in the case of other people. . . . But as for me I will abide in my chains.[71]

Why does the novel's one date happen to be 1876, the centennial year of American national independence? When patriotic Isabel calls Henrietta an "emanation of the great democracy" (Chap. 10), or when we read that "the national banner had floated immediately over" Madame Merle's birthplace, the Brooklyn navy yard, James seems to be inviting us to consider the value of independence in terms of what it means for American women. Isabel's talk about liberty has a great deal of empty posturing in it. Madame Merle is all the worse for having the "breezy freedom" of the American flag. Mrs. Touchett dries up from following "her own theory" of what makes "a good wife" (Chap. 18). *The Portrait* is a *counter*-centennial novel. It consistently shows that the sort of liberty that is manifested in institutional reform – the emancipation of women in particular – has a harmful effect on the social order. The freedom that interests James is the internal kind, where the hands remain manacled, but the spirit — somehow — spreads its wings.[72]

James betrayed Minnie Temple in *The Portrait* not because he feared or resented her. He was extremely fond of her, not only wishing her well but entering deeply into her experience, as Ralph does with Isabel. But James had been vigorously instructed by his father not to believe in Minnie's or anyone else's free intrepidity, and he himself was often passive, absorbing life at second-hand. It was just because of this spectatorial orientation that he both adored his cousin and discounted her love of liberty and the high integrity of her "pet theory." When she died, he became convinced in a moment of electrifying power that he had known a genuine overreaching heroine, one whose brilliant potential must have come to nothing, and he began thinking his way toward *The Portrait*. He figured out how to combine the precocious girl and middle-aged lover from women's fiction with his own heartless Diana and dying soldier. Yet the energizing insight that gave his imagination a once-in-a-lifetime impetus was based on a final refusal to imagine that his cousin could have survived on her own terms. James was able to write his greatest novel to date precisely by ascribing to Minnie his own private defeat, stabbing her image with the paternal steel that had been driven deep into his own soul. *The Portrait* is the book of a supreme artist in deep and unconscious subjection. That is why, in betraying Minnie Temple, James also betrayed himself. In taking over her image and then transforming her into someone so different, he transformed himself, as keeper of her flame, into the manipulative middle-aged guardian-lover he detested.

NOTES

1. *The Portrait of a Lady* (New York: New American Library, 1963), Chapter 3. Unless otherwise specified, subsequent citations are to this reprint, which is based on the first British edition (London: Macmillan, 1881). The author thanks William Veeder for criticizing an earlier version of this essay.

2. *Henry James, 1866–1916: A Reference Guide* (Boston: Hall, 1982), p. xv.

3. Henry James, *Letters*, ed. Leon Edel (Cambridge: Harvard University Press, 1974–1984), vol. 3, p. 534.

4. *Notes of a Son and Brother* (New York: Scribner's, 1914), pp. 481–2.

5. "Henry James, Jr.," *Century Magazine* 25 (November 1882): 26.

6. In *Woman's Fiction: A Guide to Novels by and about Women in America, 1820–1870* (Ithaca: Cornell University Press, 1978).

7. Henry James, *Literary Criticism: Essays on Literature, American Writers, English Writers*, ed. Leon Edel with Mark Wilson (New York: Library of America, 1984), pp. 617, 590, 189, 190.

8. "Watch and Ward," *Atlantic Monthly* 28 (August 1871): 238.

9. *Literary Criticism*, p. 637.

10. James's 1867 story "Poor Richard" had attributed the same weak reaction to its strong, independent orphan-heroine: "an immense weariness had somehow come upon her, and a sudden sense of loneliness. A vague suspicion that her money had done her an incurable wrong inspired her with a profound distaste for the care of it." *The Tales of Henry James*, ed. Maqbool Aziz (Oxford: Clarendon Press, 1973–1984), vol. 1, p. 165.

11. *Emily Chester. A Novel* (Boston: Ticknor and Fields, 1864), pp. 44–5.

12. "The Portrait of a Lady," *Atlantic Monthly* 46 (December 1880): 741.

13. *Literary Criticism*, p. 589.

14. The provisional title was mentioned as early as October 24 [1876] and as late as July 23 [1878] (*Letters*, vol. 2, pp. 72, 179).

15. The Howells letters are dated October 24 [1876] and February 2 [1877]; that to William, January 12 [1877] (*Letters*, vol. 2, pp. 72, 97, 91).

16. "The Portrait of Isabel Archer," *American Literature* 45 (March 1973): 50.

17. "Isabel Archer and the Enclosed Chamber: A Phenomenological Reading," *Henry James Review* 7 (Winter–Spring 1986): 52.

18. James, *The Art of the Novel: Critical Prefaces*, ed. Richard P. Blackmur (New York: Scribner's, 1934), p. 48.

19. The reviewer in *Penn Monthly*, possibly Elizabeth Stuart Phelps, considered Isabel "a very clever mechanical drawing of an automaton, who moves perfectly in every part, but who, after all, is not alive" (13 [March 1882]: 233). Among modern critics who stress the novel's unadmitted tendentiousness is Adele Wiseman, who argues that Isabel "is destined by the writer to epitomise and validate a particular

cultural ideal of feminine heroism" ("What Price the Heroine?" *International Journal of Women's Studies* 4 [November/December 1981]: 459).

20. James to his sister Alice, February 22 [1876] (*Letters*, vol. 2, p. 30).

21. *Literary Criticism*, p. 986.

22. December 28, 1880. All holographs of James family letters are quoted by permission of Alexander James and the Houghton Library. Edel misreads "mark" as "work," then tries to render the sentence intelligible by inserting "in" before "the work of art" (*Letters*, vol. 2, p. 324).

23. Minnie Temple to John Chipman Gray, January 7, 1869. The Temple–Gray correspondence, surviving only in fair copies made by Alice Howe James and Margaret Mary James, is quoted by permission of the Houghton Library.

24. Temple–Gray, August 29, 1869.

25. Temple–Gray, January 25, 1870.

26. Temple–Gray, January 25, 1870 and January 27 postscript.

27. "Woman's Sense of Humor," *Critic* N.S. 1 (March 29, 1884): 145–6.

28. Alice Howe James to Henry James, May 17, 1913. Alice H. enclosed the second sentence in its own quotation marks, as if to stress her accuracy in quoting it.

29. Temple to Helena de Kay, May 12 or 13, 1863. The Temple–de Kay correspondence, apparently extant only in typed copies made by Rosamond Gilder, is quoted by permission of Gilder Palmer.

30. "H. de K & Minnie Temple roomed together at school." Rosamond Gilder, binder labeled "Early Notes on H.G.'s Letters/Tyringham III." Quoted by permission of Gilder Palmer.

31. Temple–de Kay, April 3, 1863 and July 12, 1862.

32. Temple–de Kay, April 3, 1863.

33. *The Letters of Henry James,* ed. Percy Lubbock (London: Macmillan, 1920), vol. 2, p. 417.

34. May 9, 1869.

35. Information on Clymer comes from J. C. Croly, *The History of the Woman's Club Movement in America* (New York: Henry G. Allen, 1898), p. 20; J. C. Croly, *Sorosis: Its Origin and History* (New York: J. J. Little, 1886), p. 13; Grace Gates Courtney, *History: Indiana Federation of Clubs* (Fort Wayne: Fort Wayne Printing Co., 1939), p. 12; Ella M. Dietz Glynes, "The Minerva Society and Sorosis," *Woman's Journal* 35 (January 2, 1904): 2–3; and Theodora Penny Martin, *The Sound of Our Own Voices: Women's Study Clubs 1860–1910* (Boston: Beacon Press,

1987). Clymer's uncle, Robert Dale Owen, had defended liberal divorce legislation in a *New York Tribune* debate with Horace Greeley in 1860. At a meeting of Sorosis in 1871, Clymer "recited a dreadful slur on the fidelity of both sexes, called the 'Faithful Lovers' " (Anon., "Sorosis – A May-Day Meeting," *New York Tribune* [May 2, 1871]: 8). In editing Minnie's letters for *Notes of a Son,* James excised her two references to Clymer.

36. *Mary Chesnut's Civil War,* ed. C. Vann Woodward (New Haven: Yale University Press, 1981), p. 543.

37. April 24, 1869.

38. *Notes of a Son* introduces the letter containing this statement by repeating for the second time in Chapter 13 that Minnie would have found life an agony if she had lived (p. 491). Perhaps James felt that Minnie was headed for trouble.

39. Leon Edel, *Henry James: 1843–1870 The Untried Years* (Philadelphia: Lippincott, 1953), p. 252.

40. August 15, 1869.

41. *Literary Criticism,* p. 599.

42. Henry to William James, March 29 [1870].

43. Alfred Habegger, "Henry James's Rewriting of Minny Temple's Letters," *American Literature* 58 (May 1986): 166–7, 176; italics mine.

44. "A Woman in *The Portrait of a Lady,"* *Henry James Review* 7 (Winter–Spring 1986): 18–28.

45. *Letters,* vol. 2, p. 179.

46. *Ibid.,* p. 337.

47. December 17, 1882.

48. *Letters,* vol. 4, p. 707.

49. For a good conventional account of the differences between Ralph and James, see Stuart Hutchinson, "Beyond the Victorians: *The Portrait of a Lady,"* in *Reading the Victorian Novel: Detail into Form* (London: Vision Press, 1980), p. 280: "Ralph is indeed very close to James. . . . Watching Ralph perform . . . James understands how drastically more compromising it is to try to fulfill the requirements of one's imagination in life, than it is by writing a novel." Working at a time when few biographical materials were available, Ernest Sandeen (*"The Wings of the Dove* and *The Portrait of a Lady:* A Study of Henry James's Later Phase," *PMLA* 69 [December 1954]: 1060–75) pointed out some important connections between Ralph and James – their ambiguous "love" for a cousin, their assumption of control over her destiny, their struggle for health.

50. *Art of the Novel*, pp. 289–90.
51. *Tales*, vol. 1, p. 26.
52. *Tales*, vol. 1, p. 250.
53. *Henry James*, p. 234.
54. Temple–de Kay, April 3, 1863.
55. Henry James, *A Small Boy & Others* (New York: Scribner's, 1913), p. 15.
56. See Habegger's discussions of this in "The Lessons of the Father: Henry James Sr. on Sexual Difference," *Henry James Review* 8 (Fall 1986): 1–36; "New Light on William James and Minny Temple," *New England Quarterly* 60 (March 1987): 28–53; and chapter 6 of *Henry James and the "Woman Business"* (New York: Cambridge University Press, 1989).
57. Richard Brodhead puts this well: "Expressing his own most powerful patterns of consciousness in fiction . . . is precisely what James does not do in his earliest writing; instead it is what he comes to be able to do, as the result of a practical program of literary apprenticeship" (*The School of Hawthorne* [New York: Oxford University Press, 1986], p. 131).
58. *Literary Criticism*, p. 592.
59. *Tales*, vol. 1, p. 42.
60. *Letters*, vol. 1, pp. 50, 56.
61. Houghton Library.
62. This 1866 story shows how early James had a firm ideal of noble womanhood: Adela's "part was still to be the perfect young lady. For our own part, we can imagine no figure more bewitching than that of the perfect young lady under these circumstances" (*Tales*, vol. 1, p. 102).
63. *Tales*, vol. 1, p. 259.
64. *Tales*, vol. 1, p. 234.
65. *Notes of a Son*, p. 413.
66. *Literary Criticism*, pp. 598, 192.
67. "Watch and Ward" (September, December 1871) 339, 709.
68. (Harmondsworth: Penguin, 1986), p. 222.
69. (New York: Norton, 1975), p. 252.
70. Henry James, Sr., to Julia A. Kellogg, September 9, 1871.
71. H.[enry] J.[ames, Sr.], "Morality vs. Brute Instinct. Marriage vs. Free Love," *Saint Paul Daily Press* (19 February 1874): 2. Of course, Isabel doesn't live up to all of Henry Sr.'s dogmas. It's out of the question that she should redeem Osmond, and she doesn't at all submit as he

expects. But as Annette Niemtzow shows in "Marriage and the New Woman in *The Portrait of a Lady*," *American Literature* 47 (November 1975), Henry Sr.'s views "guide the last hundred pages," so that Isabel is required "to satisfy the moral code that the elder James prophesied would come if legal marriage contracts were dissolved and she does so 'freely' and 'consciously'" (380, 388). Robert White argues in "Love, Marriage, and Divorce: The Matter of Sexuality in *The Portrait of a Lady*," *Henry James Review* 7 (Winter–Spring 1986): 59–71, that James faces and resolves the problems of human sexuality by assuming his father's sacramental view of marriage.

72. See Adeline R. Tintner's discussion of James's "ironic" use of 1876 in "The Centennial of 1876 and *The Portrait of a Lady*," *Markham Review* 10 (Fall–Winter 1980–81): 27–9. Charles Feidelson's brilliantly developed argument for the tragic freedom of Isabel's consciousness has, to my eyes, an insubstantial glitter. Freedom that is merely "intrinsic" – Sisyphus' freedom in Camus' parable, Henry Sr.'s freedom in slavery – seems a rationalization for servitude. Feidelson's "The Moment of *The Portrait of a Lady*" is collected in the Norton Critical Edition of *Portrait*.

4

The Portrait of a Lack

WILLIAM VEEDER

> . . . and indeed [I] have a strong impression that I didn't at any
> moment quite know what I was writing about: I am sure I couldn't
> otherwise have written so much.
>
> —Henry James

DESPITE the evident fact that he was a male child in a family
of seven Jameses, young Henry found the truest representation of his self in the figures of the orphan and the woman. Both
figures respond to the threat of extirpation that James felt menac-
ing him from within his home and throughout his society. As a
defense against and a compensation for his situation, James engaged in a recurring fantasy which he recognized as a child, deployed as a novelist, and discussed in his autobiography. In order
to explain how this core fantasy and its attendant anxieties helped
shape his first major masterpiece, *The Portrait of a Lady*, I will begin
with the autobiographical volumes, *A Small Boy and Others* and
Notes of a Son and Brother.[1] Here James sets forth three of the most
important things represented in *The Portrait* — the negating threat
of transience and mortality, the realization that men as well as
women are marked by emasculation and lack, and the Jamesian
defenses against and compensations for such a situation. Taken
together, the autobiography and *The Portrait* help reflect James's
precarious but tenacious sense of himself, for in each text he both
manifests his sense of negativity as the prime sign of the human
condition and defines a fantasy to deal with a sense of lack so
endemic.

Core Fantasy: Defense and Compensation

A Small Boy reveals James's indulgence in what Freud would call
Family Romance.[2] "I seemed to have been constantly eager to
exchange my lot for that of somebody else" (SB 175). In Freud this
exchange involves replacing father and mother with such figures

95

as the King and Queen. Young Henry James comes closest to this
classic version of the fantasy when he describes with empathy and
even envy the Prince Imperial, the baby son of Napoleon III,
"borne forth for his airing or his progress to Saint-Cloud in the
splendid coach that gave a glimpse of appointed and costumed
nursing breasts and laps, and beside which the *cent-gardes*, all
light-blue and silver and intensely erect quick jolt, rattled with
pistols raised and cocked" (SB 332). The nursing breasts and the
cocked pistols represent well the Imperial Parents of fantasy. They
do not, however, constitute the staple of James's family romance.
His is more bizarre.

In describing a cousin, Henry exults that "this genial girl, like
her brother, was in the grand situation of having no home" (SB
188). The homeless orphan: here is the ideal. In James's negative
version of the family romance, parents are replaced not by mon-
archs but by corpses — or rather, by absences. "I think my first
childish conception of the enviable lot, formed amid these associations, was to be little fathered or mothered" (SB 14).[3] What in
Henry James would prompt so bizarre a family romance? Like all
fantasies, James's is both a defense and a compensation. So, I can
rephrase my question: what is James defending himself against?
An immediate answer is his parents. Another answer — less obvious but with finally more explanatory power — is his society.
Underlying both answers is a complex anxiety about negation
which relates orphanhood to James's sense of "woman."

To explain why young Henry would want to extirpate his parents, we must recognize the complex threat that Henry Sr. and
Mary Walsh James presented. Each parent was at once lethal and
ineffectual. The lethalness of Henry Sr. surfaces in a note in Emerson's diary. "Henry James said to me, he wished sometimes the
lightning would strike his wife and children out of existence . . . "[4]
Emerson goes on to add James's explanation: ". . . and he should
have to suffer no more from loving them." But we may wonder.
And a small boy may have wondered too. Everywhere he looked,
death was proving how ephemeral life was. "Our father's family
was to offer such a chronicle of early deaths, arrested careers,
broken promises, orphaned children"[5] that James could conclude:

"so few of those that brushed by my childhood had been other than a tinkling that suddenly stopped" (SB 77).

In the context of so transitory a family, a small boy might well wonder about a father who risked taking his five young children to Europe three times in a decade. The very ships that plied the Atlantic often went down like stones. "Since the wretched Arctic had gone down in mortal woe . . . her other companion, the Pacific, leaving England a few months later and under the interested eyes of our family group, then temporarily settled in London, was never heard of more" (SB 278). What Henry Jr. repeatedly returns to is the question of his father's very rationality. Virtually every year from the ages of six to sixteen he was placed in a different school. Phrases such as "rash failure" (SB 300), "my father's precipitate and general charity" (SB 300), "an effect of almost pathetic incoherence" (SB 302) reveal the danger a small boy sees in a paternal "optimism [which] begot precipitation" (SB 307).

Young Henry needed self-protectiveness all the more because the expectable bulwark against his father's unconscious lethalness – his mother – proved startlingly ineffectual in the face of Henry Sr.'s migratory urges. Instead of putting her foot down, Mary went along with her husband, in every sense. The danger of maternal passivity is compounded by the other side of Mary's character – the aggressiveness of her smothering attentions to Henry. His defensive response is to rearticulate in young adulthood the family romance of his childhood. When "abjectly, fatally homesick" in London in 1869, Henry longs to lie "with my head in mother's lap and my feet in Alice's!"[6] but such proximity would involve too immediate an involvement in family relations. One reason why Henry is in London is to escape the smothering mother. Mary James knows this, of course: "Your life must need this [my own] succulent, fattening element more than you know yourself."[7] What Henry knows about himself is that he must forego his cake and eat it too. So he gains *dozens* of pounds in London, then informs his mother that "I am as broad as I am long, as fat as a butter-tub and as red as a British *materfamilias*."[8] The once skinny son has thus incorporated maternal nurturance while escaping mother. London as "a good married matron" fosters "British stoutness."[9] Surrounding himself with a barrier of fat — "my flesh hangs over my waistband in huge bags"[10] — Henry keeps the world at a distance. Obesity constitutes the physical equivalent of his family romance of exclusion, especially with the Atlantic Ocean providing a supplementary moat to his wall of fat.

To the danger posed by a smothering mother and an unconsciously destructive father, young Henry James responds in kind. He negates negating threats. His family romance kills the parents before they can get to him.

But fantasies kill no one, of course. And even if they did, the threats to the small boy would not cease with the extirpation of his parents. Henry knows himself also vulnerable to forces from outside the home, from American society. In this larger realm is what I need to complete my definition of James's sense of self. The "woman" as well as the "orphan" contributes to this self-image because James is marked irrevocably by his sense of the merging of male and female. Not only are both sexes at home dangerously one in their potential to negate, but both genders in society are dangerously one in their negated actuality. James's family romance has to negate not only negating parents but also a negative cultural situation.

Let me begin with a distinction between the genders — made sometimes by James himself and formulated succinctly by Edel — which is at variance with my claim that men and women are one in negation. "Downtown was the world of the money-makers that he [James] didn't know and couldn't write about. Uptown represented leisure, largely feminine (since the males were Downtown making the money), and this world was useable in his books."[11] The word "largely" is unobtrusive in Edel's sentence, but it is enormous for James's psyche. That the majority of males in America were downtown earning money makes particularly threatening the fact that the majority of males in James's family were not. For Henry James the distinction downtown versus uptown does not square finally with man versus woman. He establishes

> that scarce aught but disaster *could,* in that so unformed and unseasoned society, overtake young men who were in the least ex-

posed. Not to have been immediately launched in business of a rigorous sort was to *be* exposed – in the absence I mean of some fairly abnormal predisposition to virtue: since it was a world so simply constituted that whatever wasn't business, or exactly an office or a "store," places in which people sat close and made money, was just simply pleasure, sought, and sought only, in places in which people got tipsy. (SB 48–9)

Business, then, means life, and pleasure means disaster. Pleasure also means "woman." After establishing "the wondrous fact that ladies might live for pleasure, pleasure always, pleasure alone," Henry focuses upon his Aunt Catherine, who "was distinguished for nothing whatever so much as for an insatiable love of the dance; that passion in which I think of the 'good,' the best, New York society of the time as having capered and champagned itself away" (SB 40). Woman is as evanescent as champagne bubbles, as transitory as waltz music. It is into this context that James introduces an emblematic couple, a doomed bride and groom. "It is at all events to the sound of fiddles and the popping of corks that I see even young brides, as well as young grooms . . . vanish untimely" (SB 42). By turning the wedding waltz into the *danse macabre,* James is saying not so much that woman is doomed as that pleasure dooms everyone – groom as well as bride. "Exposed . . . exposed" in the passage from pages 48–9 of *A Small Boy* has definitely a sexual intimation, a menace of castration. Castration here means being cut off from business, being exposed to the dangers of pleasure.

Henry James understood what recent feminist scholars have insisted upon – that gender is socially produced. When his society equates business with life, it is defining "presence" in a way appropriate to bourgeois patriarchy: "man" = business = life = presence. Thus "woman" = pleasure = death = absence/negation. This is why I say that "woman" as a gender construct is a social fate available to persons of either sex. In James's America, a male who is not in business is feminine in gender because he is signed by, is singled out for, nonexistence. "Castration" marks not the anatomically female sex but a culturally effeminated group.

Everything about young Henry James seemed to him to bespeak "woman." His principal sources of pleasure – art and Europe – lie outside American capitalism. Artistic inclinations, for example, prove as fatal as champagne to men in the James family. Cousin Bob

> seemed exposed, for his pleasure – if pleasure it was – and my wonder, to every assault of experience. . . . it was all in the right key that, a few years later, he should, after "showing some talent for sculpture," have gone the way of most of the Albany youth . . . and died prematurely and pointlessly. (SB 188)[12]

The danger inherent in an inclination to art is compounded by an attraction to Europe. Death is again the reward of pleasure as James catalogues the family fatalities. First there is "a young collateral ancestor who died on the European tour" (SB 123); then, cousin Albert, "a small New York Orestes ridden by the furies" whose "early Wanderjahre" ended as soon as he "disembarked in England. . . . He just landed and died" (SB 133, 142, 143). Cousin J. J. makes it back to New York, "but he had verily performed his scant office on earth. . . . [being one of] those to whom it was given but to toy so briefly with the flowers" (SB 192, 193).

Such vulnerability James associates expressly with his negated family's disinclination to the business career that was America's alternative to pleasure. "Disconnected from business we could only be connected with the negation of it. . . . the word had been passed, all round, that we didn't, that we couldn't and shouldn't, understand these things" (NSB 71; SB 189–90). So familywide a lack characterizes the small boy inevitably. "I never dreamed of competing – a business having in it at the best, for my temper, if not for my total failure of temper, a displeasing ferocity" (SB 176). The word "business" here does not mean commerce specifically, but its appearance in James's sentence underscores his commercial insufficiency. Competition *is* business in bourgeois capitalism, so that James's refusal to compete signifies his refusal of the downtown world of men. "My own aptitude showing for nil" (SB 325), Henry fills *A Small Boy* with his failures.

Here is where the ineffectuality of Henry James, Sr., proves most threatening to his namesake. Father, who should stand forth as patriarch, as embodiment of culture, becomes in the James family the supreme articulation of the negative and negated. Staying up-town with the women – and marked as physically lacking by the amputation of his right leg – Henry Sr. with his "almost eccentrically home-loving habit" (SB 72) seemed to his son to be effeminated, "afraid to recognize certain anxieties, fairly declining to dabble in the harshness of practical precautions or imposition" (SB 72, 200). Lack characterizes the patriarchal portrait. "That the head of our family was *not* in business" struck the small boy as "tasteless and even humiliating" (NSB 71); that his father espoused no organized religion meant that "our pewless state . . . involved, to my imagination, much the same discredit that a houseless or a cookless would have done" (SB 234); that Henry Sr. "cared only for virtue that was more or less ashamed of itself" (SB 216) meant that he was compromised even as a moralist.

With the patriarch of the family marked so stringently by lack, young Henry James finds at home no defense against the negating effects of American society. If business = life, and if inadequacy in business (and/or a commitment to "pleasure") = death, then James can defend against such inadequacy only by denying his inept father – and by extension all relationships that might link him to the fatal world of pleasure. Henry Jr.'s core fantasy of extirpation articulates the defense that he enacted throughout his long life: no intimacies. As he remained devoted to parents and siblings but kept an ocean between himself and "home," so expatriation enabled him to maintain immediate contact with Anglo-American society while remaining safe from exposure. The assurance that "I should be an eternal outsider"[13] in London meant that relationships there could never be intimate enough to threaten him seriously. What biographers and critics have duly noted – that James assumes the onlooker's position – is most poignant when we recognize that distanced observation is the practical implementation of his family romance fantasy.

More needs to be said, however. A defense is also a compensation. Granted that home life taught young Henry James both sexes could be actively lethal and passively dangerous; that social life taught him all people who were not "in business" were "feminine" in gender; and that in each case, domestic and social, James's defense was to negate negativity – he derived important positive compensations from such negating. James was far more alive to experience – more affirmative in responses, more resilient in meeting setbacks, more daring as an artist – than my pages so far (and than *A Small Boy and Others*) would indicate. James's family romance partakes of and contributes to his determination to live. It functions as a compensation because it says that, however many others in the family have succumbed to transitoriness, *he* has survived. Telling himself a story thus helps Henry James to enact his life. Even as a small boy he believed deep down, deeper than anyone at the time could guess, that *he* was marked by presence, that he had a productive genius denied to his father. Eschewing intimacies was the price he felt he had to pay to exercise his talent.

In addition to this general compensation provided by lifelong orphanhood is the specific compensation derived from the second figure in whom James saw himself represented – "woman." An often-noted fact about James's fiction – that he expresses the aggressive, daring aspects of himself more through his female characters than through his male – is possible precisely because of the way woman was produced in American society. Freedom and daring of mind (and even of action) characterized the American girl long before she debuted in James's fiction. In the society around him, in other words, young Henry James saw not only active male figures who could never express his self but also active female figures who could. He particularly needed a compensatory affiliation with the feminine because he had to defend against one additional threat from home.

The purest form of James's family romance was not the genial girl's, for she was not completely free. She was encumbered by a brother. James's ideal is "still another of the blest orphans" (SB 120), cousin Albert.

> If it was my habit, as I have hinted, to attribute to orphans *as* orphans a circumstantial charm, a setting necessarily more delightful than our father'd and mother'd one, so there spread about this appointed comrade [Albert], the perfection of the type, inasmuch

as he alone was neither brother'd or sister'd, an air of possibilities that were none the less vivid for being quite indefinite. (SB 120–1)[14]

Thus young Henry fantasized about extirpating not only his parents but also his brothers and sisters. Most threatening was inevitably William James, the dauntingly brilliant and frequently punitive elder brother. Defense and compensation were particularly needed here, for William was much loved.

Henry's erotic inclinations toward William have been suggested by various biographers.[15] If we grant that the younger brother was "in love with" the older, what are the causes and the effects of this emotion? Causation in Henry's case seems virtually paradigmatic of homosexual object choice as Freud defined it: a son prevented – by paternal ineffectuality and maternal oversolicitude – from accomplishing the Oedipal transfer from mother to father seeks men for two reasons. On the one hand, his failure to bond with father means that the boy remains joined to mother and thus desires what she desires – men. The most dominating male presence in Henry's immediate view was the dynamic William. On the other hand, the son who has failed to affiliate with the father lacks a role model and thus seeks perpetually a masculine figure to incorporate as the ego ideal which would solidify his conception of himself as masculine. Again William stands forth conspicuously. What complicates the paradigm, of course, is that the male chosen by Henry abides *within the family*. To one taboo – homosexuality – is thus added another – incest. A young man already wary of all relationships will of course repress such desires, but he must deal with the narcissism involved in loving someone who is both of his sex and in his family. If solipsism is obviously the danger of Henry's family romance of negation – of obliterating everyone but himself – the addition of narcissistic object choice only worsens matters. James's salvation comes from telling himself stories – about women.

In the year of William's marriage, 1878, Henry began to write novels about heroines instead of about heroes. If passive Henry, already "feminine" in his self-perceived negation, functions as "the girl" in his unconscious homosexual bond with active William, he becomes the girl rejected, the woman scorned, when William weds. Henry compensates by projecting his female self outwards: he enacts through his fiction what no longer works as private fantasy. Moreover, the change in Henry's narrative pattern coincides with the other major changes of 1878. His enormous gain in weight occurs precisely at this time, the fall and winter of 1878–79. Henry is using body as well as art to buffer himself against the shock of William's rejection. Body could never compensate enough, however, given a sensibility as creative as Henry James's. He must tell himself a story, over and over. How he uses fiction-as-fantasy to enact the orphaned-woman-as-lack we can see in his first major masterpiece.

Portrait of a Lad(d)y

When Henry James was eight years old, he endured in the studio of the famous photographer Matthew Brady a portrait session described, like so much in *A Small Boy*, in terms of negation. "Sharp again is my sense of not being so adequately dressed as I should have taken thought for had I foreseen my exposure" (87). Again there is the threat of "exposure," emphasized this time by the photography pun. James never exposed himself in fiction so vulnerably as he did in Brady's headbrace. *The Portrait of a Lady* contains much autobiographical data, but it also contains traps for any unwary equator of life and art. Edel in his discussion of cousin Minny Temple's tuberculosis maintains that "she became, nine years after her death, the heroine of *The Portrait of a Lady*."[16] There is indeed a death from tuberculosis in *The Portrait*, but the victim is Ralph Touchett. Isabel Archer evinces traits of Minny, as she does of Henry James, but Isabel is *not* Minny, any more than she *is* Henry. The small boy who grew up too wary of exposure to entrust himself to any one personal relationship became a novelist careful to avoid one-to-one correspondence with any character. Studying *The Portrait* as autobiography is useful precisely because it requires us to see how diverse James's self-representation is, how many characters reflect him. His "problem [of how] to live in England, and yet not be of it" (Chap. 5) challenges Daniel Touchett; his awareness that parents attempt to atone through their children for their own lives having "failed so dreadfully" (Chap. 51) is dramatized with Pansy; the "selfishness" inherent in "the preference for a single life" (Chap. 29) marks Gilbert Osmond; and the Jamesian fear of "exposure" is expressed through three women. Isabel feels "the fear of exposing – not her ignorance; for that she cared comparatively little – but her possible grossness of perception" (Chap. 24); Lydia Touchett parodies James's fussiness about his health when she affirms "her wisdom in not exposing herself to the English climate" (Chap.5); and Pansy's sense of the inadequacy of her dress recalls James's anxiety at Matthew Brady's as she asks Merle, "'why should I expose it beside your beautiful things?'" (Chap. 25).

James's self-portrayal in *The Portrait* achieves coherence not because of any one-to-one correspondence with life, but because of the consistency with which he represents what we saw in *A Small Boy* and *Notes* – the negating threat of transience and mortality, the fact that men as well as women are marked by emasculation and lack, and the Jamesian defenses against and compensations for such a situation. Attention to these essential matters will, I hope, enable us both to gain new insight into a complicated novel and to confront the notoriously difficult end of *The Portrait* in a way which will help account for – though by no means explain away – its difficulties in terms of James's core fantasy of negation.

The Portrait opens with the threat of transience. By its very placement in midafternoon, the "ceremony" of tea becomes part of, rather than a bulwark against, the flux of time. "The shadows . . . long upon the smooth, dense turf . . . lengthened slowly" (Chap. 1) – inexorably. By the time Isabel awaits the death of the tea ceremony's host, "the shadows [have] deepened" (Chap. 18). She has just met Madame Merle, whose introduction of Gilbert Osmond will darken life still more. "Then the shadows began to gather; it was as if Osmond deliberately, almost malignantly, had put the lights out one by one" (Chap. 42). Isabel's final scene in *The Portrait* begins amid "shadows [that] were long upon the acres of turf" and ends in "darkness" (Chap. 55). The flux of time is reflected in transient lifestyles. As children, Ned, Ralph,

Isabel, Merle, Gemini, and Gilbert were all whisked – like the James children – back and forth across the Atlantic and around the continent. As adults, Lydia, Merle, and Ned continue their restless search for pleasure, while Henrietta roves professionally, Caspar and Warburton pursue Isabel, and Ralph flees death. James's international theme derives not simply from his knowledge of the expatriate community in Europe, but from his realization that expatriation represents the human condition of transience.

The association of transience with mortality which we have seen in *A Small Boy* recurs in the opening of *The Portrait*, as flux leads to death. The mortal illnesses of Daniel and Ralph Touchett sign them as negated from the start. Daniel "was not likely to displace himself," Ralph "was not very firm on his legs" (Chap. 1). The fact that disease is established before love enters the novel is important: fatal women do not cause male inadequacy in *The Portrait*.[17] Warburton may suggest such causation when he tells Isabel, "'if you refuse me . . . I shall live to no purpose'" (Chap. 12), but Warburton has had no purpose from the first. Though he seems healthy next to Daniel and Ralph, Warburton too is sick. "'He is sick of life'" (Chap. 1). Warburton's negation is political, for "'he doesn't take himself seriously . . . and he doesn't know what to believe in. . . . [he] can neither abolish himself as a nuisance nor maintain himself as an institution'" (Chap. 8). Warburton admits "'I don't approve of myself in the least'" (Chap. 14). The fact that political negation constitutes, in effect, the condition of "woman" is confirmed when Warburton goes on to equate himself, however ironically, with his powerless sister. "'We neither of us have any position to speak of'" (Chap. 14). Association with another powerless woman is prepared for in the first scene, where Warburton wears "a hat which looked too big for him" (Chap. 1). Pansy too wears a "hat [which] always seemed too big for her" (Chap. 35). That "'she does not really fill out the part'" (Chap. 37) is equally true of Warburton, as Isabel confirms. "'I said she [Pansy] was limited. And so she is. And so is Lord Warburton'" (Chap. 40).

That emasculate men inhabit the condition of the feminine is confirmed in the opening description of the tea drinkers. "They

were not of the sex which is supposed to furnish the regular vo-
taries of the ceremony" (Chap. 1). In the face of woman's traditional definition as the nonmale, men here in *The Portrait* are
defined as the nonfemale – *at the very moment that the females are
marked as absent.* Lydia, who should preside over the tea ceremony,
is not here; Isabel, who could substitute for her, has not yet arrived
on the lawn. To be the negative of the absent does not give presence to men, for the lengthening shadows emblematic of mortality
"were the shadows of an old man sitting . . . and of two younger
men strolling" (Chap. 1). Transience and consequent negation are
epitomized by one of the shadows, Ralph Touchett, who "'does
nothing.' . . . there was really nothing he had wanted very much
to do, so that he had given up nothing" (Chap. 5). That men
reduced to Ralph's "'mere spectatorship'" (Chap. 15) are worse
off, are less than, women is emphasized by Madame Merle. "'A
woman, perhaps, can get on. . . . But the men . . . what do they
make of it over here? I don't envy them, trying to arrange themselves. Look at poor Ralph Touchett . . . "an American who lives
in Europe." That signifies absolutely nothing'" (Chap. 19). Negated like Ralph are his servant, who "'is good for nothing; he is
always looking out the window'" (Chap. 54); Mr. Luce, who "was
the most unoccupied man in Europe, for he not only had no
duties, but he had no pleasures" (Chap. 20); and Ned Rosier, who
"'can't go home and be a shopkeeper . . . can't be a doctor . . .
can't be a clergyman . . . can't be a lawyer'" (Chap. 20). Most
important, and possibly most surprising, Ralph is like Gilbert Osmond. "'He does nothing' . . . 'I could do nothing' . . . 'What is
he? Nothing at all but a very good man. He is not in business'"
(Chaps. 10, 24, 32). Our difficulty in distinguishing Ralph from
Gilbert (who is the subject of all the clauses here except the first)
has its counterpart when Daniel Touchett says of his son what
proves true of Osmond: "'You look at things in a way that could
make everything wrong'" (Chap. 18). We readers agree of course
with Isabel's distinction "that Ralph was generous and her husband was not" (Chap. 42), but this distinction must be earned in
the face of important similarities between the two men.

These similarities, moreover, implicate expatriate women as well.

Both genders in *The Portrait* negate life by turning persons into objects. This reifying penchant, which is unmistakable in Osmond – he defines Isabel as "'a young lady who had qualified herself to figure in his collection of choice objects'" (Chap. 28) – also characterizes Ralph, who initially sees Isabel as "'a Titian, by the post, to hang on my wall'" (Chap. 7). Long before Osmond asks Merle "'what do you want to do with her'" (Chap. 22), Ralph asks Lydia "'what do you mean to do with her . . . what do you mean to do with her . . . what do you mean to do with her . . . what [do] you intend to do with her?'" (Chap. 5). Though Ralph's mother responds properly – "'Do with her? You talk as if she were a yard of calico'" – Lydia is already tarred with her own brush. "'For a woman of my age there is no more becoming ornament than an attractive niece'" (Chap. 5). That Isabel is an object for women as well as for men is evident when Ralph celebrates spectatorship.

> "I shall have the entertainment of seeing what a young lady does who won't marry Lord Warburton."
> "That is what your mother counts upon too," said Isabel.
> "Ah, there will be plenty of spectators! We shall contemplate the rest of your career."

The "gaze" is not exclusively masculine in *The Portrait,* as it is in so much of Western culture.[18] When Merle says to Isabel, "'I want to see what life makes of you'" (Chap. 19), she foresees direct entertainment for Osmond and indirect profit for herself. Both sexes are unable *not* to treat human beings as objects because both sexes sense their own essential reification. Without a positive sense of one's own subjectivity, one cannot value the other as subject, as sacredly *other.* Being essentially negated is what expatriation represents for both sexes. "'If we are not good Americans we are certainly poor Europeans; we have no natural place here'" (Chap. 19).

Isabel attempts to maintain traditional sex divisions when she asserts that "'I am not an adventurous spirit. Women are not like men'" (Chap. 15), but in fact no one in *The Portrait* is "like men." Everyone is "woman" because no one is truly "adventurous."[19] No one can get beyond the mere spectatorship which marks Ralph and mars Osmond. Gilbert's litany – "'I have neither fortune, nor

fame, nor extrinsic advantages of any kind' " (Chap. 29) — is echoed by Merle: " 'What have I got? Neither husband, nor child, nor
fortune, nor position, nor the traces of a beauty which I never
had' " (Chap. 19). Distinctions of sex vanish in a wash of negatives
as relentless in *The Portrait* as in *A Small Boy.*

> "I never do anything," said this young lady (Chap. 14) . . . "I don't
> come up to the mark" (Chap. 15) . . . "you will be sure to take no
> one who is not" (Chap. 16) . . . It passes, like everything else . . .
> "No; the best part is gone, and gone for nothing" . . . "What have
> my talents brought me? Nothing but the need of using them
> still" . . . The dreams of one's youth . . . Who had ever seen such
> things come to pass?. . . no tears, no sighs, no exaggeration (Chap.
> 19) . . . Nothing tender, nothing sympathetic . . . no wind-sown
> blossom, no familiar moss (Chap. 21) . . . "I teach nothing" . . . "I
> wish I could give you something that would last" . . ."You don't
> care" . . . "No; I don't think I care much" (Chap. 22) . . . He
> seemed to intimate that nothing was of much consequence (Chap.
> 24) . . . "There are no good ones [husbands]" . . . "there is noth-
> ing, nothing, nothing" (Chap. 25) . . . "I have nothing on earth to
> do" . . . "I am afraid Bantling was ashamed of me" (Chap. 27) . . .
> she fell in love now-a-days with nothing (Chap. 40) . . . "I have no
> friends . . . No one would do for me what you have done for her"
> (Chap. 44) . . . "He does nothing. But he doesn't like me" (Chap.
> 47) . . . "If I don't know you, I know nothing" (Chap. 49) . . . "Do
> you mean that without my *bibelots* I am nothing?" (Chap. 50) . . .
> "he wouldn't miss her if she were removed" (Chap. 51) . . . "It has
> not been a successful life." (Chap. 54)

The spirit which prompted James's core fantasy prompts Ralph
Touchett to say " 'I think I am glad to leave people' " (Chap. 54).

Having defended against the threat of extirpation by engaging as
a small boy in the fantasy of orphanhood, James as an adult enacts
this fantasy by filling *The Portrait* with orphans. In addition to
Warburton, who "had lost both parents" (Chap. 8), and Henrietta,
who is "without parents and without property" (Chap. 6), there is
Ned, whose mother is never mentioned and whose "father was
dead and his *bonne* . . . dismissed" (Chap. 20); Merle, who never
refers to her mother and praises her father in the past tense (Chap.
18); and Gilbert and Gemini, whose "mother had died three years

after the Countess's marriage, the father having died long before" (Chap. 26).[20] It is left to Isabel to articulate that attractive potential of orphanhood which James fantasized about in his family romance. She achieves the status of James's chief autobiographical resource in *The Portrait* because she knows the *attraction* of negation, an attraction which the other characters can never know because they are defined absolutely *as* negated. Isabel says, "'I belong quite to the independent class. I have neither father nor mother'" (Chap. 16).

The freedom of orphanhood is associated in *The Portrait* with another obsession of *A Small Boy* – as Isabel goes on to say, "'I am poor.'" She experiences the Jamesian opposition between business, which necessitates restrictions, and pleasure, which promises liberation. This opposition originates in her life precisely where it did in Henry's own. Her father too exhibits "occasional incoherency of conduct" (Chap. 4). Isabel represents that very isolation from the world of money which marked the children of Henry James, Sr. Since business is "everything" in America, Isabel, like Henry James, Jr., is inevitably characterized by "nothing":

> Isabel of course knew nothing about bills. . . . "I don't know anything about money." . . . "She has nothing but the crumbs of that feast [her father's spending of his capital] to live on, and she doesn't really know how meagre they are." (Chaps. 3, 18)

Economic naivete is only one aspect of Isabel's psychic economy, however, because she functions in *The Portrait* as more than a replication of Henry James. She is also the wish-fulfillment which assures him compensation. Isabel is thus endowed with a childhood free of the anxiety over paternal incoherence and financial uncertainty which scarred Henry's own youth. "If he [Mr. Archer] had been troubled about money matters, nothing ever disturbed their [his children's] irreflective consciousness of many possessions" (Chap. 4). Wish-fulfillment then persists into adulthood. Isabel avoids the financial anxieties that James knew in his twenties and early thirties because *The Portrait* presents – apparently – a fairy tale solution to such anxieties. First a good witch whisks Isabel away to Henry's cherished refuge, England. Then an ideal father-surrogate absolves her of all financial worry. Isabel has achieved material independence without having to grub for it in business.

What makes the ending of *The Portrait* so difficult is that wish-fulfillment proves finally incompatible with fairy tale. If James were writing a storybook romance, the now-rich princess would marry her prince charming and live happily ever after. Instead Isabel marries disastrously. To understand how such an anti-fairy tale can function compensatorily as a wish-fulfillment for Henry James, we must understand why his protagonist chooses a prince *un*charming. "'I am marrying a nonentity . . . a person who has none of Lord Warburton's great advantages — no property, no title, no honours, no houses, nor lands, nor position, nor reputation, nor brilliant belongings of any sort. It is the total absence of all these things that pleases me'" (Chaps. 32, 34). Part of the attraction here is Isabel's power to launch Gilbert's boat, the "maternal" power to *make* him, which many critics have noticed. But as the words "nonentity" and "absence" and all the negatives indicate, there is more involved. Or rather, less.

Osmond is for Isabel the quintessence of absence, the essential nullity. And why would that attract her? "Of all liberties, the one she herself found sweetest was the liberty to forget" (Chap. 21). Here is where the freedom of the orphan leads ultimately: not to action but to *nada*. James knows well the limitations of his family romance of extirpation. It is at best a local, provisional solution, because the ultimate threat is not external, not familial or even social, but internal. What is mortal about us is our own mortality; we will die even if no one kills us. Thus for a person obsessed with vulnerability, the only way to deal with the fear of being killed is to kill it. This means to kill the self. In the animal world, the dog bites the wounded paw that is wounding him; in the human world, thanatophobia leads to suicide. Isabel Archer expresses Henry James's desire to escape from suffering altogether. Gilbert Osmond constitutes the ultimate *nada*. He has expressly defined his life to Isabel as a negative surrender. "'Not to worry — not to strive nor struggle. To resign myself'" (Chap. 24). That these words do not in fact characterize competitive, emulous Gilbert is irrelevant to Isabel's charmed reception of his words. What Gilbert offers her is what she wants, negation. And she is willing to pay a high price for it. "It was *not* that, however, his objecting to her opinions; that was *nothing*. She had *no* opinions − *none* that she would *not* have been eager to sacrifice in the satisfaction of feeling herself loved" (Chap. 43, my italics).

Thus when we see Isabel mastered by negativity after her marriage − "there was nothing to gape at, nothing to criticize, nothing even to admire" (Chap. 39) − we must not jump to the melodramatic conclusion which Ned reaches and which Isabel tries to persuade herself of: that this is all Osmond's doing. Of course he has sought a certain type of "nothing" in his wife. But Isabel too has sought "nothing." The tragedy, almost the comedy, is that they have not meant the same thing by nothing. Negatives saturate the portrait of Isabel after her marriage:

> she appeared now to think there was nothing worth people's either differing about or agreeing upon (Chap. 39) . . . she was resolved to assume nothing . . . she would recognize nothing (Chap. 41) . . . she answered nothing . . . She answered nothing (Chaps. 41, 42) . . . Nothing was a pleasure to her now (Chap. 42) . . . "I have heard nothing of it" . . . Isabel could say nothing more; she understood nothing; she only felt that she did not know her husband yet (Chap. 50) . . . "I have guessed nothing . . . I don't know what you mean" (Chap. 51) . . . "I don't know why you say such things! I don't know what you know." (Chap. 52) . . . Nothing seemed of use to her to-day . . . She asked nothing (Chap. 53) . . . "I never thanked you − I never spoke − I never was what I should be!" (Chap. 54)

We would succumb to the temptation to blame Gilbert for Isabel's negation if we were to ignore the fact that the desolating negatives which proliferate after her marriage derive not simply from that marriage but from the years of her life before it. Isabel has always been afraid − of knowing.

> "I don't know − I can't judge" (Chap. 2) . . . "I don't know what you are trying to fasten upon me, for I am not in the least an adventurous spirit. Women are not like men." (Chap. 15) . . . "She doesn't know what to think about the matter at all" (Chap. 20) . . . "I don't want to know anything more − I know too much already"

(Chap. 24) . . . "I would rather hear nothing that Pansy may not!"
(Chap. 35)

Fear of knowledge involves what James fears most – exposure.
"'A large fortune means freedom, and I am afraid of that. . . . I am
not sure that it's not a greater happiness to be powerless'" (Chap.
21). Isabel is speaking specifically about her fear of making good
use of her money, but the larger fear and the larger issue is of
freedom itself, the orphan's legacy. It necessitates exposure, it
flaunts those very risks against which James's virtually pathological sense of vulnerability defends. Gilbert Osmond as negation is
the ultimate defense against and compensation for the negating
forces of experience.

He is also more. He is compensation for the terrible year of 1878.
To indulge through *The Portrait* his homoerotic love for William,
Henry must do more than switch from male to female protagonists
and invest Isabel with aspects of himself. He must also project
aspects of William onto Gilbert. This is easy enough to do, for in
his most recent big novel, *The American* (1877), Henry had already
portrayed unflattering aspects of his elder brother, both in the
coldness of the elder Bellegarde, and (as William himself recognized)[21] in the hypercritical morbidity of the little American tour-
ist, Rev. Babcock. The recurrence of these features in Osmond is
not therefore surprising. What is startling is how much more obvious and extensive the portrait of William becomes by 1881.

> He was a man of forty, with a well-shaped head, upon which the
> hair, still dense but prematurely grizzled, had been cropped close.
> He had a thin, delicate, sharply cut face, of which the only fault was
> that it looked too pointed; an appearance to which the shape of his
> beard contributed not a little. (Chap. 22)

Born in 1842, William James is on the threshold of forty in 1881.
Although his hair would not grizzle until later, the other features
of Isabel/Henry's portrait of Gilbert are accurate enough. The well-
shaped head; the hair cropped close; the face thin, delicate, and
sharply cut; its pointed quality emphasized by the beard: these
features are all suggested in the two illustrations I have included –

William James, 1865

the photograph from 1865 and the self-portrait (sans beard) from about 1868. In body type, William shares Gilbert's "light smooth slenderness of structure" (Chap. 24). The intellectual acuity of each man is signaled in "his luminous intelligent eye" (Chap. 22). And temperamentally, William as well as Gilbert "was certainly

114

William James, self-portrait sketch, c. 1868

fastidious and critical" (Chap. 24). Isabel adds to her portrait that "he was *probably* irritable" (Chap. 24, my italics) because she does not know *yet* what her creator had already suffered from for years – how punishingly irritable William's fastidiously critical sensibility could be. What the younger brother said about the elder in the very year of the composition of *The Portrait* – "he takes himself and his nerves and his physical condition too seriously"[22] – is said about Osmond in the novel. "'He takes himself so seriously'" (Chap. 34).

Probably most aggressive is Henry's implication of William in one other trait conferred upon Osmond. "'In itself your little picture is very good. . . . But as the only thing you do it's so little' " (Chap. 22). Both William and Gilbert are amateur painters of some talent. By denying to Gilbert all true creative genius, Henry can take revenge upon the artistic and scholastic superiority that William flaunted throughout their school years. The genius evident in *The Portrait* allows Henry to take the high ground here. And high ground is essential for wish-fulfillment. As the woman scorned by William, Henry expresses through Isabel a double triumph. Her marriage to Osmond is the realization of Henry's courtship of William, while the public revelation of Osmond's marital failure constitutes Henry's revenge upon the one who had failed him by marrying another.

More than such nastiness is involved, however. The year 1878 confirmed Henry James in renunciation: there were no more intimate relationships that he could or would risk. For *The Portrait* to function as truly compensatory wish-fulfillment, James must handle not only Isabel's marriage to and rupture with Osmond, but also her life afterwards. She must walk the narrow line between two types of negation presented in the novel. She must avoid the deadening lovelessness of Gilbert, Merle, and Lydia, who end up cut off from life; yet she must not succumb to the deadening self-effacement inherent in unions like Warburton's with " 'Lady Flora, or Lady Felicia — something of that sort' " (Chap. 54). To effect the ultimate wish-fulfillment, James returns Caspar Goodwood to the stage of Gardencourt.

For all his phallic puissance, Caspar too is marked by lack:

> "There *is* nothing left for Mr. Goodwood" . . . The future had nothing more for him . . . He was hopeless, he was helpless, he was superfluous . . . "I have nothing else to do" . . . "I can't understand, I can't penetrate you" . . . Mr. Goodwood . . . was quite as sick, in a different way, as Mr. Touchett. (Chaps. 48, 51)

Sick no less than the sexually dysfunctional Ralph and the politically problematic Warburton, Caspar has not learned *The Portrait*'s lesson about negation. He holds to patriarchal stereotypes which credit the male with presence and reduce the woman to absence. Having said early on that " 'an unmarried woman — a girl of your

116

age – is not independent. There are all sorts of things she cannot do' " (Chap. 16), Caspar continues at the end to give the negative constructions to Isabel and now bestows the positive on himself. "'You don't know where to turn. Now it is that I want you to think of me. . . . You don't know where to turn; turn to me!' " (Chap. 55). What Caspar offers Isabel is a future not of sexual liberation but of perpetuated inequality. Freedom is not the watchword here, because the absence of any truly egalitarian viewpoint characterizes Caspar's empty rhetoric. He emphasizes his paternalism by incorporating Isabel into that exchange of women which Lévi-Strauss defines as the origin of patriarchy – "'he [Ralph] left you to my care . . . '" Caspar for his sins then becomes the butt of something close to outright sarcasm from the Jamesian narrator: " '. . . my care,' said Goodwood, as if he were making a great point" (Chap. 55).

Freedom abides finally for the adult Isabel where it did for the orphan Henry: not in relationships, but in isolation. What is usually said about Isabel's final state is that "she has gone back to her husband." In fact, *The Portrait* ends not with Isabel having gone back to her husband, but with her *going* back. By setting the last scene of the novel on the morning of Isabel's departure from England – rather than, say, on the next day, when she would already have reached Rome – James leaves his protagonist suspended between departure and arrival, poised between separation and commitment. Isabel is neither with the pair who represent the bondage of advocated adultery – Caspar and Henrietta – nor with the pair who represent the bondage of conventional domesticity – Gilbert and Pansy. Isabel is alone, yet not solipsistic, neither exposed nor dead. Her train ride is a timeless suspension. Like the figures on Keats's Grecian urn, Isabel is preserved in midmotion: " . . . do not grieve; / She cannot fade . . . forever young; / All breathing human passion far above" (ll. 18–19, 27–28). In her railway coach Isabel enters this state on her ride out to England.

> To cease utterly, to give it all up and not know anything more – this idea was as sweet as the vision of a cool bath in a marble tank, in a darkened chamber, in a hot land. She had moments, indeed, in her journey from Rome, which were almost as good as being dead. She

sat in her corner, so motionless, so passive, simply with the sense of being carried, so detached from hope and regret, that if her spirit was haunted with sudden pictures, it might have been the spirit disembarrassed of the flesh. There was nothing to regret now – that was all over. (Chap. 53)

Freud called it the Death Drive, the organism's determination to return to the condition of nonexistence. But suicide cannot be countenanced as the resolution of either James's novel or his family romance. "'Dear Isabel, life is better; for in life there is love. Death is good – but there is no love'" (Chap. 54). Henry James believes this. Thus his lifelong dilemma is Isabel's now: how to love, and yet maintain enough distance to escape the exposure inevitable with intimacy; how to remain in life, but not of it.

On the train ride out to England Isabel had not yet rejected Caspar and thus had not yet confirmed her rejection of the adultery which would be suicide for her. The ride back, however, is different. Through his formal artistry James achieves the compensation that his life could never provide. Art assures both that Isabel's train will never arrive and that her acts of commitment to life, love, and relationships – to Pansy, on behalf of marriage – will suffice as a rejection of suicide and a commitment to life. Like Ralph, she can do without the people, yet unlike Ralph she is saved from the death feared by Henry James and us all.

Like Sigmund Freud, who studied our species' drive toward death, James explores our instinct for exclusion and reclusion. He attests to this instinct's strong operation within himself so that we readers will have to recognize what our world of marrying and begetting is determined – in its own wish-fulfillment – to pretend away. Our unions are rarely more than mutual violations. When Henrietta says to Ralph, "'You are not in love with her [Isabel], I hope,'" and he quips "'how can I be, when I am in love with another,'" Henrietta speaks to us all when she snaps, "'you are in love with yourself, that's the other'" (Chap. 13). That each person wants to be both lover and beloved in order to deny the very possibility of any true other is a self-negating propensity which Henry James chronicled more extensively, fiercely, delicately than any novelist in our language. If life, like Isabel's Rome, threatens to end up "nothing but a void full of names" (Chap. 28), James's portraits of "nothing" help fill that void with an enduring presence.

NOTES

1. Henry James, *A Small Boy and Others* (New York: Charles Scribner's Sons, 1913); *Notes of a Son and Brother* (New York: Charles Scribner's Sons, 1914). All subsequent references to these volumes will be included in the text, preceded by the abbreviation *SB* or *NSB*. Since my argument is oriented to James's life at the time of the composition of *The Portrait*, I have used the 1881 version of the novel. All quotations are taken from the Signet edition (New York: New American Library, 1963).

2. Sigmund Freud, "Family Romances," in *Collected Papers*, ed. James Strachey (New York: Basic Books, 1959), vol. 5, pp. 74–8. For more recent studies of family romance see R. C. Bak, "Discussion of Greenacre's 'The Family Romance of the Artist,'" *Psychoanalytic Study of the Child* 13 (1958): 42–3; Helen K. Gediman, "Narcissistic Trauma, Object Loss, and the Family Romance," *Psychoanalytic Review* 61 (1974): 203–15; Phyllis Greenacre, "The Family Romance of the Artist," *Psychoanalytic Study of the Child* 13 (1958): 9–36; Linda Joan Kaplan, "The Concept of the Family Romance," *Psychoanalytic Review* 61 (1974): 169–202; Christine Van Boheemen, *The Novel as Family Romance* (Ithaca: Cornell University Press, 1987).

3. James returns obsessively to the idyllic state of the orphan: the "rare radiance of privation" experienced by cousin Gus (*SB* 173), "the undomesticated character at its highest" enjoyed by cousin Bob (*SB* 188).

4. Ralph Barton Perry, *The Thought and Character of William James* (Boston: Little, Brown, 1935), vol. 1, p. 3.

5. James repeatedly specifies his various fated cousins: Minny Temple, "radiant and rare," was "extinguished in her first youth" (*SB* 13); cousin Gus Baker, "as by a sharp prevision, snatched what gaiety he might from a life cut short" (*SB* 172); cousin Vernon was "the most interesting surely in all the troop of our young kinsmen early baffled

and gathered" (*SB* 389); Vernon's sister too was doomed "prematurely to die" (*SB* 395), like the Pendleton's "so sturdily handsome, little boy" (*SB* 377) and like J.J.'s sister, who "confirm[ed] the tradition, after all, by too early and woeful an end" (*SB* 193). James's own vulnerability to self negation is evident in his response to the famous taunt of his brother William ("'I play with boys who curse and swear!'"): "I had sadly to recognize that I didn't, that I couldn't pretend to have come to that yet. . . . It wasn't that I mightn't have been drawn to the boys in question, but that I simply wasn't qualified" (*SB* 259, 260).

6. Leon Edel, *Henry James. The Untried Years: 1843–1870* (Philadelphia: Lippincott, 1953), p. 284.

7. Ibid., p. 47.

8. Leon Edel, *Henry James. The Conquest of London: 1870–1881* (Philadelphia: Lippincott, 1962), p. 343.

9. Edel, *Untried Years*, pp. 295, 419.

10. Edel, *Conquest of London*, p. 343.

11. Edel, *Untried Years*, p. 103.

12. "Exposed" also is "another slim shade, one of the younger and I believe quite the most hapless of those I have called the outstanding ones . . . succumbing to monstrous early trouble after having 'shown some talent' for music" (*SB* 189).

13. Edel, *Conquest of London*, p. 270.

14. For other references to orphanhood in *SB* see pp. 15, 129, 189, 402. Other James children reflect interestingly upon Henry's obsession with orphanhood. Wilkie expresses the classic family romance fantasy when he says "'I became quite convinced by the time I was twelve years old that I was a foundling'" (Jane Maher, *Biography of Broken Fortunes* [Hamden, Conn.: Archon Books, 1986], p. 12).

15. James's homosexual inclinations were first given serious treatment by Edel in connection with the novelist's relationship with the Scandinavian sculptor Henrik Anderson in the 1890s (*Henry James. The Treacherous Years: 1895–1901* [Philadelphia: Lippincott, 1969], pp. 306–16). In 1979, Richard Hall traced these inclinations back to the 1870s in connection with Henry's relations with his brother William ("An Obscure Hurt," *The New Republic*, April 28 and May 5, pp. 25–31 and 25–9). For an intelligent examination of the forces which produced Henry James's homosexual inclinations see B. D. Horwitz's essay, "The Sense of Desolation in Henry James," *Psychocultural Review* 1 (1977): 466–92.

16. Edel, *Untried Years,* p. 331.
17. Though men definitely express fear of women in *Portrait* (Chaps. 4, 9, 10, 13, 48), women as well fear men (Chaps. 48, 49), and they fear one another (Chaps. 9, 49).
18. For a lucid discussion of Freud's making the gaze a phallic activity (in "The Uncanny") and the response of French feminism to such gendering see Toril Moi's *Sexual/Textual Politics* (London: Methuen, 1985), pp. 134–5, 180n.
19. Two exceptions might seem to be Henrietta and Caspar. Both, however, are unable to sustain their adventurousness. Isabel's disappointment at Henrietta's succumbing to marriage is supported by the name James gives to Henrietta's fiancé – "Bantling" means "baby." Caspar is active at the factory and would have been valiant on the battlefield. But love for Isabel makes fantasy life meaningless, and Caspar was – significantly – born too late to fight in the Civil War.
20. No mention is made of Caspar's mother; his father is referred to in ways which make it unclear whether the factory proprietor is still alive (Chap. 13).
21. Perry, *Thought and Character,* vol. 1, p. 371.
22. Edel, *Conquest of London,* p. 419.

5

Frail Vessels and Vast Designs:
A Psychoanalytic Portrait
of Isabel Archer

BETH SHARON ASH

O NE psychological characteristic of nineteenth-century literature is the occultation of the mother. James's *The Portrait of a
Lady* displays its family resemblance to other novels and auto-
biographies of the period by assuming that the relation between
father and child (son) is at the center of the universe of human
development, love, and autonomy, and by obscuring the relation
between mother and child. That James observes this convention,
and at the same time writes a mimetic text about a woman, is a
curious situation. Isabel proudly proclaims that she has neither
father nor mother, that she makes herself; but it is Isabel's mother
(not her father) who is scarcely mentioned and who seems to have
been excised from the novel. Since the development of female
subjectivity depends, first of all, on a maternal identification, the
feminist reader is compelled to ask what James has done with
Isabel's mother and how this maternal absence shapes Isabel's
dream of self-fashioning. Since the mother cannot be effaced
unproblematically, and since erasure in this case is a strategy of
closure at both the level of character and the level of narrative
performance, an intriguing possibility arises: perhaps the mother's
absence serves as the submerged organizing principle of the text.

For Isabel, the desire to establish a potentially autonomous ego
becomes an urgent, though unknowing, response to the absent
mother. This is a provocative claim. James's portrait of Isabel has
been widely understood as a creative response to his own literary
fathers, primarily Emerson and Hawthorne. Leon Edel reads the
novel as "a critique of American 'self-reliance' ";[1] and John Rowe
delineates specific parallels between Hester Prynne and Isabel

Archer — that both are proud isolationists forced by experience to accommodate their ambitions to narrow worlds and, in the process, compelled to repair broken connections between past and present (Hester) or between America and Europe (Isabel).[2] Also, Edel and Rowe agree that *The Portrait* is a conventional Bildungsroman. What remains unexplored by such readings, however, is the simple fact that the novel is about a woman who has suffered maternal deprivation. In several distinguishing ways, *The Portrait* is a portrait of female psychology under patriarchy — or, more specifically, of the narcissistic and submissive tendencies typical of women trying to cope with a culture defined largely by the dominance of male desire. One result is Isabel's self-alienation. Mistaking Osmond's desire for her own, Isabel becomes an accomplice in her own oppression. Isabel's misfortune, exchanging as she does a largely illusory freedom for a marriage of reciprocal objectification, is a fate with peculiarly female dimensions. While not discounting the importance of literary fathers, I believe that a largely formalist approach misses some highly relevant facts: James is a psychological novelist; *The Portrait* is a psychological novel about an isolated *female* subject; and James knew all too well that the anxiety of maternal influence is at least as important as paternal literary influence. Critical readings which neglect these elements are diminished by their repetition of a Victorian (and pre-Freudian) view of psychology that elides the mother.

James's attitude towards mothers was decidedly ambivalent. Though on the occasion of his mother's death he extolled her as an example of saintly devotion, he invariably represented mothers in his fiction as manipulative, self-centered, and often terrifying. Perhaps his fictional mothers were never endowed with the selflessness he attributed to his own mother *because* he knew all too well that a selfless mother could make selfishly illegitimate demands. Jean Strouse claims that because "Mary James gave her children all, they owed her nothing less than everything."[3] Hated for many of the same reasons she was loved, Mary James exacted a debt of guilt for her fiercely angelic sacrifices. While it is not my purpose to argue clear connections between James's biography and his fiction, the life does not contradict, and might even support, the possibility that the mother's absence in *The Portrait* is not innocent (a mere absence). It is entirely possible that her banishment encodes both a consummate image of maternal selflessness *and* a lack of positive maternity.

Viewed psychoanalytically, the force of the absent mother arises from a complex aggregate of primitive (pre-Oedipal) maternal images. The individual's dependence on a mother who is absolutely necessary to survival inspires two abiding but contradictory images of omnipotent maternity, one all-gratifying, and the other all-depriving (the two faces of the "phallic" mother). Modification of this primitive love by a realistic sense of the mother as a female subject – a process which normally occurs during childhood and adolescence – is absolutely necessary to productive emotional life. When, as in *The Portrait*, the mother remains a morbid source, an account eternally held in abeyance, she survives most powerfully in the child's psyche in the form of these two absolute and contradictory images (the one all good, the other all bad). Absent, the mother cannot provide the continued involvement that would give the child a capacity to relate to others without overlaying these relations with the terrible ambivalences of the primal maternal legacy – that is, with fantasies of maternal power which cannot know each other, and which ultimately prevent the child from negotiating the complexities of adult life.

That Isabel defends against fantasies of maternal power by attempting to forget altogether things associated with her disappointed beginnings is suggested by the pain she feels when remembering even pleasant aspects of her past. "It was in her disposition at all times to lose faith in the reality of absent things; she could summon back her faith . . . but the effort was often painful even when the reality had been pleasant" (1908 version, Chap. 21). Such faithless recollection of her past, and failure to recognize its determining importance in the present, leaves Isabel free to entertain the central illusion of her youth: that she can make and remake herself through acts of will. It is highly ironic that her progress through the novel, haunted by unintegrated psychological images from the archaic past (the two faces of the maternal imago), should be obstructed by an insistent linkage be-

125

tween passive forgetting and the aggressive voluntarism implied by willing oneself to be perpetually new.

Isabel's failure of memory leads to expressions of self that leave her neither here nor there: "'I don't know whether I succeed in expressing myself, but I know that nothing else expresses me'" (Chap. 19). As a critic of optimistic individualism (self-reliance), James implies that his heroine's inexpressible individuality is really a mystified attempt to make the ego an end in itself. Isabel's glorification of free egoic creation is an unhappy "solution" to particularly American problems: a new mobility in relations with others, and an instability or democracy of values, both of which promote a conception of the individual ego as principal arbiter of human experience. American ego psychology stresses adaptive functioning rather than determinism, autonomy defended and clearly defined rather than unknowable subjectivity. However, according to the French psychoanalyst Jacques Lacan, adaptive egoism is actually the seat of narcissistic illusion. We are neither entirely our own masters nor are we blessed with the infinite capacity to master the world, for "in the last resort [our identifying formulas] are to be understood only in reference to the truth of 'I am an other.'"[4] Lacan's poetic formula describes subjectivity as a process and not an entity; to the extent that the subject relies on the support of a falsely unified self-image, he fails to recognize that desire is not in service to the ego at all, and thereby short-circuits subjectivity by reinforcing only defensive (egoic) claims.

Since Americans and American ego psychologists[5] valorize the adaptive function of the ego, they are poorly positioned to appreciate James's insight that American "normalcy" tends toward narcissistic pathology. In this context, Isabel might even be thought of as a representative "adaptive" narcissistic ego. But the specifics of female psychology under patriarchy complicate any simple claims for or against Isabel's normalcy. Whether deemed ordinary, remarkable, or deviant, her life is above all tragic: for Isabel, acts of rationalized submission are the only alternative, and really no alternative at all, to narcissistic illusions.

I will begin by exploring the possibility that James's refusal to acknowledge the importance of a girl's relation to her mother elevates this relation to the position of a controlling absence. Then, in the second section, Isabel's egoic armor will be seen as a formidable defense against powerful desires; her dread of sexuality fends off a fearsome pre-Oedipal dependency. The description of Isabel's "narcissism" developed in the course of this analysis will help to unlock the problem of her union with Osmond. I will argue that the marriage trap is set and submitted to because it represents a resumption of pre-Oedipal conflict and bears witness to the return of the "phallic" mother. In sum, Isabel's problematic egoism refers the reader back to an unrecollected beginning, a maternal absence which, once uncovered, helps to answer the central question of the novel: how and why does Isabel Archer, so independent, full of desire and desirable, end up confined to a conjugal prison cell?

The Genealogy of Motherhood

Successful psychological maturation has been traditionally understood as a resolute turning away from the mother toward the authority of the father. In *Insight and Responsibility*, Erik Erikson describes the normative paradigm of development as a move "from dependence to self-help [and self-esteem], from women to men, [and] from perishable to eternal substances."[6] Enculturation in patriarchal society provokes the subject's defensive scorn of the mother, a reactive response which guards against intrinsic feelings of helplessness and insufficiency associated with the child's absolute reliance on the mother. The psychoanalyst Janine Chasseguet-Smirgel sees the story of the goddess Athena as one of escape from primal dependency, her flight as a denial of origination: "There is no mother anywhere who gave me birth."[7] *The Portrait* enacts a similar defensive gesture, but now through a psychologically complex character in a mimetic fiction which attentively demonstrates the human consequences of both absence and denial. Behind its overt representations of "successful" developmental norms (patriarchal self-idealizations based on concealments of the mother), the text traces a maternal presence-in-absence too absolute, too carefully ensured by James to ignore.

127

The maternal lacuna draws attention to itself early in the novel by a peculiar transcription: Mrs. Lydia Touchett's famous telegram announcing Isabel's arrival at Gardencourt. It reads: "'Changed hotel, very bad, impudent clerk, address here. Taken sister's girl, died last year, go to Europe, two sisters, quite independent'" (Chap. 1). As Ralph comments, his mother's telegram admits of multiple interpretations because she has "'mastered the art of *condensation.*'" Ralph is not, of course, characterizing the mechanism of the dreamwork as later described by Freud; yet apparently unconscious textual superimposition of the two parental deaths is integral to the telegram's message. Consider the series, "Taken sister's girl, died last year, two sisters, quite independent." Isabel's father is clearly the parent who died last year; but Mrs. Touchett, the sister of the dead Mrs. Archer, seems to refer to *Mrs. Archer's* death, thus allowing for a telegrammatic slip that emphasizes Isabel's mother's absence. Ambiguity also surrounds the identity of the sisters. Does Mrs. Touchett refer to Isabel's two sisters, Edith and Lillian, or to herself and Mrs. Archer? If the reference also inadvertently points to the dead mother and her sister (Mrs. Touchett), then another meaning (other than the reference to Isabel) should be given to the word "independent." Because Isabel's mother had made an imprudent match in Mr. Archer, a marriage which required Mrs. Touchett to curtail all relations with her sister, these "two sisters" had led lives independent of one another. Thus, the dead mother peeks into the text telegrammatically – by way of condensation.

This ambiguity should not be stressed to the neglect of a second confusion in the telegram, this one concerning Mrs. Touchett's relation to Isabel. In addition to unconsciously touching on the absent mother's death, Isabel's aunt also unwittingly refers to Isabel's death in the phrase "Taken sister's girl, died last year, go to Europe." According to Mrs. Touchett, Isabel is quite dead *as her mother's daughter.* After invoking Mrs. Archer's death, Mrs. Touchett unconsciously replaces her. The switch is ensured by the fact that Isabel's resurrection depends on Mrs. Touchett's sponsorship, which rescues her from the Albany house where "a great many people have died" (Chap. 3). Isabel's emergence from America to

Europe is rather like her being reborn from out of the head of Mrs. Touchett. Aunt Lydia is Isabel's best imaginative ally in the project "to begin afresh" (Chap. 4), but the mixed messages in her telegram belie its practical tone. Absence invades even the sparest factual account (the telegram) of Isabel's new beginnings.

Mrs. Touchett, who might have acted maternally toward Isabel by comforting her for the loss of both parents, shows a greater regard for real estate than for emotional relations. According to Mrs. Touchett's plan, Isabel's inheritance of the Albany house might be the occasion of considerable profit. She tells her niece: "'They'll probably pull it down and make a row of shops. I wonder you don't do that yourself'" (Chap. 3). But neither Aunt Lydia's entrepreneurial officiousness nor her conscious refusal to indulge regrets or speculations can render Isabel independent of her past. Financial provision is not the same as emotional guidance, nor is real estate a substitute for familial identity. For Isabel to renew herself, to be born into adulthood, she must also make peace with the sorrows of her childhood, which include the absent mother. Since the text is our (and Isabel's) only memory of what came before, the mother's exclusion amounts to an exclusion from both Lydia's and Isabel's remembrance; and unremembered, the original loss cannot properly be mourned. Does Isabel, like Mrs. Touchett, want to consign regrets over Mrs. Archer to irrelevance?

Does Isabel, in other words, repress her mother's death and so transform it into an unmournable absence, thus dangerously precluding any positive maternal identification? It is likely that the absence of the mother makes positive identifications with femininity and acceptance of maternity rather difficult. As if to demonstrate the psychological pitfalls awaiting willful females, the text reveals a genealogy of disrupted relations between women.

Isabel is allowed at once to submit to and avoid her own motherhood: her only child is given and taken away in the space of a sentence. A fact much overlooked is that the baby Isabel has with Osmond is mentioned only once, and then only after his death. It is also significant that with Isabel's assumption of motherhood, Mrs. Touchett again refuses a sisterly identification with her. Though Mrs. Touchett's son Ralph is dying – it is a time in the lives of both women when they could give solace to one another as bereaved mothers – Mrs. Touchett simply announces her isolation from Isabel: "'Go and thank God you've no child,' said Mrs. Touchett, disengaging herself" (Chap. 55). Isabel has nothing to give her; her anxiety at responding to a mother who is governing and emotionally lacking is simply too great. Mrs. Touchett seems to Isabel like "the matron of a gaol" (Chap. 54) – stiff, white, and cold, like a regal corpse. There is no hope here.

When Isabel turns to Madame Merle for companionship, she judges the older woman's emotions to be "historic" – shadows of the past, mere shapes of feeling (Chap. 19). Merle's remaining real sentiment is not for Isabel but for her own daughter Pansy, the child she has had with Osmond but cannot acknowledge. In taking Osmond from his first wife, Madame Merle was unfaithful to her own husband and thus obliged, after Pansy's birth, to renounce her motherhood and leave the child to Osmond's care. Osmond and Madame Merle employ the dead woman as a convenient fiction to conceal adultery and thus legitimate Pansy's birth.

Once again, the mother is hidden from view: both Madame Merle and Osmond's first wife are perpetuated as false mothers; true maternity is never represented. The elliptical structure is paradigmatic. Like Isabel, Pansy is made the daughter of a dead mother whose absence is preserved; a mother, moreover, who is replaced by a father – one who is himself idealized by his daughter. Pansy and Isabel thus double one another, as do their respective mothers: both dead, both carefully effaced by fictions. Also, Madame Merle assumes the explicit role of criminal (devalued) motherhood, mother as thief, perhaps even as murderer. She has stolen from the dead only to restore what was taken in the name of the father and at the expense of the maternal. By masking the original theft and legitimating her child, Merle makes herself the bearer of a permanent deprivation, a desire that can never be met. Thus, the general lack of positive female identification (due to the systematic *absenting* of the mother by patriarchy) is projected or externalized in Merle in the form of an ensnaring malignity: vicious in her desire to have, to be what she cannot, she manipulates Isabel without love, and becomes an empty functionary in service to the dominant code. Isabel seems to acknowledge the wound she shares with Pansy, their shared vulnerability to Merle's voraciousness, when she delivers the novel's most pointed understatement: "'You [Pansy] must never say . . . that you don't like Madame Merle'" (Chap. 52). One wonders if the command is made out of compassion or out of fear of the consequences. "Don't, whatever you do, give your mother reason to hate you," she seems to say; "she can destroy you if she will."

Isabel's Narcissism

In *The Portrait,* Isabel's self-sufficiency is an explicit theme, the absent mother an implicit one. Positive mothers or mother surrogates are clearly absent, and illegitimate mothers who fail to repair their daughter's initial loss are very much present. How then shall we read this combination of the lack of maternal care and the daughter's independence? First, it must be remembered that psychological causation is integral to James's project. Psychoanalytic theory tells us that a problematic need for self-sufficiency often arises from maternal insufficiency, and frequently is a function of an underlying narcissism. It follows that Isabel Archer, troubled champion of her own independence, might be read by the light of an appropriate understanding of narcissism and female development.

In the psychoanalytic view, among the many possible consequences of maternal deprivation, one likely result is the girl's attempt to gain confirmation from others by becoming precocious. Helen Deutsch observes that in some female adolescents who are overly dependent on praise, the "push toward maturity in one direction is linked with deprivation in another."[8] Such a girl becomes largely intolerant of unpleasure; she uses the external world as a substitute source of gratification.

Isabel's sense that "people were right when they treated her as if she were rather superior" is supported by virtually every figure in her childhood (Chap. 6). She need not display actual accomplishments to convey the "general idea" of her superiority – others invent her brilliant activities for her and almost never impede her wishes. Isabel basks in the bright light of her paternal Aunt Varian's high opinion: Isabel was "a prodigy of learning" who, according to (her Aunt's) rumor, "was writing a book" (Chap. 6). Isabel's self-gratifications are connected with an intolerance for frustration: "It seemed to her often that her mind moved more quickly than theirs, and this encouraged an impatience that might easily be confounded with superiority" (Chap. 6). Isabel decides for herself that she will not attend school. Despite "the pain of exclusion" from her peers, the important result is immediate freedom – something magical, self-given, and realized without parental prohibitions; and her pedagogical emancipation allows her to indulge the "uncontrolled use of a library full of books" (Chap. 3). Thus she is able to maintain a good standing in the eyes of others, without having to grapple with the necessary problems and pleasures of more normal maturation. Even in her youth, Isabel's independence can be seen as an evasion of normal relations with others.

Lacan's view of pre-Oedipal narcissism speaks directly to this confusion of self-love and admiration. Love is important to personal development for several reasons, but primarily because it bestows "recognition" or narcissistic confirmation – the other's acknowledgment of one's ego. The ego is an imaginary structure which reflects and distorts reality, creating multiple identifications, and thus establishing what the subject *takes to be* himself. Infantile and infantilizing adult love perpetuates the child's inability to discriminate between himself and others. In effect, "I" might be another, but "I" might not want to be informed of my misperception: the other is "I" – if and when and to the degree that "I" choose. In this narcissistic position, the ego's mechanisms of defense attempt to eliminate the frustration of the desire to be recognized, the failure of others to valorize the ego absolutely. In optimal development, the mother supports the subject but frustrates the egoic demands; only then can the subject relate to others and not use them merely as supports for the ego. It is evident, however, that the ego can counteridentify with the frustrating mother: by identifying with the threat, the ego makes a desperate effort to control it. The result, Guy Thompson explains, is the "denial of his desire for the mother's recognition" (though the object is not relinquished)

132

and the substitution of his own illusion of self-esteem. Thompson asserts that there is a "conflict between the child's desire for a lost object and his omnipotent enslavement to his ego, which now becomes the foundation for that ambivalent aggressivity which inhabits his relations with others."[9] Fear of the mother's aggression becomes fear of one's own, and relatedness becomes a temptation to aggression's unthinkable release.

Freud tells us, "The impulse of cruelty arises from the instinct for mastery."[10] Lacan extends the insight by explaining that through aggressive mastery, the subject strives to project a "unified" (illusory and alienated) image onto the world. Aggression gives rise not only to tension in the subject (as rival to himself), but also to tension between his ego and others, and to basic fears about his own integrity which limn every effort to become the ego he desires to be. For women in particular, aggression is traditionally incommensurate with self-idealization. Chasseguet-Smirgel stresses the "spiritualized" character of female sexuality as a defense against the destructive aspects of erotic life. When the cruel aspects of the maternal imago are present in a female identification, Chasseguet-Smirgel believes, serious damage is done to the girl's self-esteem.[11] By identifying with the threatening mother, the girl attempts to affirm herself (a responsibility the mother fails to take up), and thereby entrenches the ego's narcissism – its assumption of the (m)other's proper role through a psychological program of self-sufficiency.

Thus, the ego resists anything which would diminish it, including the aggressivity intrinsic to self-mastery, and solicits the collusive confirmation of others. Self-idealizing egoic images are arrayed defensively against the individual's aggressive emotions. Moreover, the narcissistic organization of the ego and its mechanisms of defense define a double-bind: the self is dependent on others for recognition and satisfying relations, but the ego (an armor of defensive structures) prevents one from establishing positive relations with others.

This psychoanalytic scheme begins to describe the relation between a conflicted maternal identification and the narcissistic mechanisms of defense designed to repair the mother's failure to affirm the child's quest for a unified image. Isabel, I believe, has just such a need to compensate for maternal failure – to manage the fact that nurture was replaced in early childhood by deprivation. The result is a burning need for narcissistic self-sufficiency, for her own superiority and independence. Other probable consequences might also be introduced. Isabel longs for pre-Oedipal satisfactions she never fully had, yet guards against the memory that her desire was not (and will not be) recognized by the mother, and does so by identifying with the frustrating maternal absence. Thus, Isabel's "narcissism" might be conceived of as a breakdown in female adolescent development. Her conflictual female identification remains unresolved, and this impairs further Oedipal growth.

The novel offers some biographical information which helps clarify the emotional undependability of Isabel's childhood world. Isabel's father, failed and profligate but nevertheless the one on whom she most relied, died in her late adolescence. Her mother is hardly mentioned, the occasion of her death never specified. Though intermittently cared for by a grandmother who was more innkeeper than parent, "a gentle old landlady who sighed a great deal and never presented a bill" (Chap. 3), Isabel is otherwise both spoiled and neglected by numerous nursemaids and governesses (Chap. 4). Out of these vaguely presented familial substitutions and involvements, Isabel formulates two basic but contradictory desires: her "unquenchable desire to please" (Chap. 4) and her "unquenchable desire to think well of herself" (Chap. 6). Neither desire, we are told, can ever be satisfied. Insatiable desire is of course a perpetual frustration, and healthy development includes learning to modify infantile yearnings and to channel desire toward salutary relations with others. Unmodified, primordial desire points to psychological impasse.

Isabel's "unquenchable desire to think well of herself" (a thought inspired in part by her father's vision of her) protects a fragile ideal. Only a studious anxiety keeps her from the taint of error, the full realization of imperfection. The struggle is plainly described in Chapter 6, where we are given the specifics of Isabel's self-ruminations:

She had an infinite hope that she should never do anything wrong. She had resented so strongly, after discovering them, her mere errors of feeling (the discovery always made her tremble as if she had escaped from a trap which might have caught her and smothered her) that the chance of inflicting a sensible injury upon another person, presented only as a contingency, caused her at moments to hold her breath. That always struck her as the worst thing that could happen to her. On the whole, reflectively, she was in no uncertainty about the things that were wrong. She had no love of their look, but when she fixed them hard she recognized them. It was wrong to be mean, to be jealous, to be false, to be cruel; she had seen very little of the evil of the world but she had seen women who lied and who tried to hurt each other.

A striking sequence of emotions is discovered in the unfolding psychic logic of this passage. There is Isabel's fear of making a mistake, her exaggerated sense of possessing a capacity to harm others, her inability to control error (even the anxiety associated with its prospect) or the inevitable guilt that follows it. Her sensitivity to inflicting "a sensible injury upon another" – as if this were a malicious trick played by her organism against the finer part of her nature, which does not expect it – is poignantly felt: "that always struck her as the worst thing that could happen to her." Subsequently, women are introduced into the meditation as if quite naturally, not only as the primary agents of emotional injury, but also as those who hurt each other. Thus Isabel ponders her own aggression and attempts to isolate herself from it – first simply by holding her breath, then by distancing herself from other women, who have become the bearers of malice. She avoids their unkindness. What Isabel fears most, the thought that suffocates, would seem to be female aggression and the capacity to provoke it – which is to say, she fears her own simple humanity. Envy and thoughtless cruelty are dangerous to Isabel's psychological survival.

The reason Isabel denies her aggression might be condensed into one word: "(s)mother." Her fantasy of her mother as a smothering trap (a fantasy of engulfment) is an expression of primal helplessness and maternal omnipotence. Isabel cannot overcome the one who inflicted narcissistic injury except by denying her own retaliatory hatred. She is inordinately sensitive to her own tendency toward emotional violence. Better that she turn aggression back upon herself in the form of self-constraint than express it openly towards others, particularly others invested with dangerous parental power. By identifying with the psychological aggressor, the frustrating mother, Isabel serves herself in two ways. First, she holds in check her own provocative aggression against the mother; and second, she patches her own injured self-esteem, her helplessness, by appropriating to some degree the punitive power she imagines her mother enjoyed over her. Isabel now controls her *own* emotions, but only by virtue of her fantasy of punishment – which is to say without generosity. She identifies with maternal restraint in order to deny its extreme opposite – maternal suffocation. In the condensed metaphor, Isabel and her mother are inextricably superimposed; Isabel's self-mastery really means incorporation of the controlling mother, whose stern vigilance becomes the standard of virtue.

This psychological program exemplifies in rough but plain outline the contours of Isabel's narcissism. Her predicament follows the paradigm of female adolescent narcissism given by Moses Laufer, who observes that the adolescent fear of aggression represents a threatening wish to retaliate for lack of gratification from the mother. "The only source of [self-esteem]," Laufer continues, "is through a complete submission to the demands of the superego," which helps both to repress the sense of inner badness and to create a feeling of self-sufficiency.[12]

This regime of self-monitoring is evident throughout the novel. To insulate herself from the angry impulses which women characteristically turn against each other, Isabel must, we are told, "be absorbed in [herself]" (Chap. 21); her project of self-creation involves "planning out her development, desiring her perfection, observing her progress" (Chap. 6). Even she realizes that she "look[s] at life too much as a doctor's prescription" (Chap. 21) – as if life necessarily implies illness, that vague sense of something wrong at the start which requires remedy, reorigination. It is certainly true that life for nineteenth-century women often implied sexual illness: desire did not merely provoke errors of feeling, but was imagined itself to be an error. The novel lends this truism remarkable specificity. Isabel's sense of womanhood as illness cannot be understood apart from the abiding influence of maternal insufficiency. Her education in "femaleness" means managing the unintegrated maternal identification as well as her own frustration and sense of helplessness.

Understanding the maternal legacy also allows the reader to better understand Isabel's relation to her father. At first the novel's overt representation of her past leads one to think that Isabel's idealization of her father is psychological bedrock; but the archaic maternal imago must also determine to some extent Isabel's paternal idealization. According to Chasseguet-Smirgel, the female subject's relation to the Oedipal father is changed by a primal (unintegrated) identification: there is, she explains, a transfer to the father of all the attributes of the "good" mother as "a mechanism of defense aimed at escaping the dangerous relation with the phallic mother by establishing a relation with the father."[13]

In the novel, the "good" mother is, in part, projected in the form of the permissive and pleasurable world of Isabel's childhood, given to Isabel by her father: "She had had the best of everything, and in a world in which the circumstances of so many people made them unenviable it was an advantage never to have known anything particularly unpleasant. It appeared to Isabel that the unpleasant had been even too absent from her knowledge. . . . Her father had kept it away from her" (Chap. 4). But Isabel's father is notoriously undependable. He is a flimsy vessel for the important job of bearing, preserving, and making viable an already damaged maternal goodness. Isabel cannot acknowledge her father's inadequacies emotionally, though she understands them intellectually. They must be "negated," as Freud says, or rationalized away, for criticism would mean turning the wrongness Isabel feels inside herself (the bad maternal identification) against her father. Instead of becoming sexually and verbally aggressive towards her father, Isabel idealizes him, substituting herself as the heir and redeemer of his impotence. This reactive denial of paternal undependability leads to the daughter's belief in her father's imagined goodness and her self-gratifying illusion of emancipation from the fetters of infancy and the recollection of loss.

Consequently, Isabel becomes for her father "his clever, his superior, his remarkable girl" who makes restitution for his lack of success. After his death, Isabel invents an ideal father. "Her handsome, much-loved father," though better able to avoid the sordid and unpleasant in aspiration than in actuality, is frankly excused by Isabel as "too generous, too good-natured" toward what was ugly – presumably, his own vices. His best apologist, she is able to assume pride in her parentage – that is, in her father's goodness – that extends even beyond the grave. "Since his death," we are told, "she had seemed to see him as turning his braver side to his children" (Chap. 4).

Isabel's narcissism is necessarily bound up with her egoic images and internalized ideals (from which egoic images draw strength). One of her most important constructions, reinforced by other characters in the novel, is her independence. She tells Caspar Goodwood:

> "I'm not in my first youth – I can do what I choose – I belong quite to the independent class. I've neither father nor mother; I'm poor and of a serious disposition; I'm not pretty. I therefore am not bound to be timid and conventional; indeed I can't afford such luxuries. Besides, I try to judge things for myself; to judge wrong, I think, is more honorable than not to judge at all." (Chap. 16)

Isabel's brief autobiography leads Goodwood to observe privately that "there was something ominous in the way she reserved her option" (Chap. 17). And the negative series – "I'm not," "I've neither," "I'm not bound," and "I can't afford" – does seem to endow the passage with a sense of foreboding. Hegel once said that the death of parents is the life of children, and Isabel would interpret this general notion quite literally: my parents are absent so that I can be present. Because she has "neither father nor mother" she is not bound to be a nonentity. She denies the debt of existence and predicates her own self-esteem on the nonexistence of others. "Independence" is thus a defensive trope: an exaggerated representation, implying a fictive overthrow of parental influence, and dependent on the narcissistic aggression which it masks. The elimination of frustrating parents coincides with an announcement of strength which, properly read, is also a confession of weakness: I have no filiations. The ego, self-incarnated potency, is cut off from the elements that structurally determine it, and is thus empty at the core. The result is a radically condensed, contradictory fantasy. For Isabel has transmuted parental lack and deficiency into her own autonomy. Having cleansed any stain of profligacy, neglect, or absence from the notion of independence, she is justified in pursuing her own desire. The narcissistic ideal circularly sanctions its own pursuit.

When Isabel explains herself by declaring (above all else) *what she is not*, Caspar Goodwood is vaguely apprehensive. On the occasion of his proposal of marriage, in the sitting room of Pratt's Hotel in London, Goodwood says to Isabel (with far-seeing suspicion): "'One would think that you were going to commit some atrocity'" (Chap. 16). Perhaps he senses her deep but disavowed aggression, sees the capacity to wound that she so strictly denies in herself but fears in women generally, and which (while not exactly destining an ingenue to a life of crime) might tempt her to turn heterosexuality into an opportunity for psychological violence – for hurt inflicted without knowledge. Refusing Goodwood's first proposal, Isabel responds to his open expression of desire with a feeling of "disgust." He has made himself hopelessly rigid and stupid; his desire, like an armament that limits him forever, repels her. He was, we are told, "naturally plated and steeled," but only by the force of wanting her.

Desire so forthrightly expressed is for Isabel a sign of vulnerability; and in her manipulation of Goodwood's proposal, a positive sexual moment for him, she exploits that desire. She sees him as a threat to be avoided, and any inclination to "open" herself to him is denied. His response, "'I disgust you very much,' said Caspar Goodwood gloomily" (Chap. 16), elicits her guilt; and this too must be expiated. Sending Goodwood away, Isabel must restrain her excitement by adopting "an attitude of devotion" – as if she had to propitiate unseen presences by atoning for "the enjoyment she found in the exercise of her power" (Chap. 17). She controls his desire, while subjecting her own to a process of rarification; she must transform her desire into a cruel response, and then assuage her guilt before she can be ready, finally, to enjoy it. Even then, desire gains in power only to limit her: her armor is a constraining disaffection that processes the needs of others to her own ends. Any effort to seek a solution to her narcissistic detachment would risk her only source of stability – self-sufficiency. Freedom is wedded to isolation, and narcissism shows itself to be a double-bind: a closed, self-perpetuating system.

This process of rarifying her own desire is motivated in part by the great dread that passion holds for Isabel throughout the novel. For example, in response to Osmond's most forceful declaration of love, she recalls similar moments, such as Goodwood's proposal, and "the dread of having . . . to choose and decide." The narrator reflects: "What made her dread great was precisely the force which, as it would seem, ought to have banished all dread – the sense of something within herself, deep down, that she supposed to be inspired and trustful passion. It was there like a large sum stored in a bank – which there was a terror in having to begin to spend. If she touched it, it would all come out" (Chap. 29). Not merely errors of feeling, but also "inspired and trustful passion" arouses her suspicion. Her need – the bank of desire which cannot be touched without bankruptcy – is great, and her ability to control it, imagined as an emptying out, uncertain. To desire actively means to acknowledge an empty space, a lack. Laufer explains that female adolescents still living under the shadow of the archaic mother often assume a passive, prepubescent relation to the body, "as if the vagina can only become safely integrated as part of the sexual body on the condition that the active search for pleasure [orgasm] is renounced."[14] For Isabel, the fear of narcissistic impoverishment is as much tied to the prospect of active heterosexuality (the unconscious fear of pleasure as harmful) as it is to the ambivalent desire to be cared for (the dread of submission, and the desire for passive unconflicted indecision). Her reactive stressing of independence – a narcissistic detachment from active desire – shields her from the anxiety engendered by her emotional demands even as it makes her behavior somewhat artificial. Her prophylactic approach to men also gives the impression (to her and to others) that there is more there, a great deal more, that requires protecting. But as we have seen, the difference between that great wealth of feeling and an empty vault may be no more than the turn of a key: in a single moment of weakness, the illusion of substance might vanish into nothing at all.

As Osmond says, in order to fascinate, Isabel need only turn men down: mere refusal is a sign of power. Indeed, Isabel has qualified for Osmond's admiration "by declining so noble a hand" as Warburton's (Chap. 28). In saying this, Osmond articulates a central strategy of sexual relations in "the phallic economy": fascination depends on not betraying one's own, and yet inciting another's, desire. We are told that "[his own] habitual system . . . was to be unexpressive exactly in proportion as he was really intent" (Chap. 46).

A feminist approach readily fits this strategy (of protecting one's own while using another's desire) into a more general critique of the phallic economy. The cultural demands of "femininity" require a woman to function as the primary signifier of desire – the phallus, an invested image of power and wholeness. All value and value transfer is thus derived from the demands of masculine desire. In the social masquerade, where there is only one form of desire, men hold the monopoly on value. A woman should be good at pretending she has "the phallus" – that is, at promising a mystical wholeness and then withholding the gift, becoming the vessel for male fantasies of female perfection and spite.[15] A radically divided femininity thus becomes institutionalized, with women made to fit one of two alternating roles: asexual mother and sexual profligate or whore.[16] From a feminist perspective, the circle of female narcissism begins with the dominant male pathology (the infantile fixation on the good/bad phallic mother) which underlies the phallic economy, defines women to themselves, and teaches them their limited options both as sexual beings and as active players in the game of desire. The lessons learned often include dissociation from one's desire, and identification with another's desire. The coquette is ever aware that her desirability rests on a promise – the promise of prized possession.

Isabel refuses to pander intentionally to male conceits, but in scorning the coquette's false performance of real desire, she reveals more plainly the fundamental nature of her own narcissistic detachment from her deepest needs. She does not uphold the standard mystifications of desire, but only because she cannot engage desire (whether her own or another's) at all; she would instead remain dissociated, fresh, forever innocent and independent of desire's danger. Her refusal is neither a sexual ploy nor an act of feminist resolve, for it is based on unconscious sources of inhibition. One of the novel's most poignant ironies is that Isabel's singularity, and the basis of her great appeal, is really a paralysis of being – that she can neither satisfy nor purposefully unmask male desire. Neither this nor that, she becomes all things to all admiring gazes. Her promise is more complex than that of the disingenuous woman, more remote and childlike, and more completely illusory.

Desiring to aggrandize Isabel's exorbitance (so that her largesse would also redound to him as her lover), Warburton asserts, "'You strike me as having mysterious purposes – vast designs,'" and adds, "'You can't improve your mind, Miss Archer . . . It's already a formidable instrument. It looks down on us all; it despises us'" (Chap. 9). Warburton is right – Isabel shuns the attachments she needs. But her insularity, which inspires his admiration, allows him to project onto her his own desire, and then to expect her affirmation of this illusion of a shared eminence.

Isabel's response to Warburton is typically evasive. By reducing his appeal to a sign in a conventional social order, she keeps his demand at a distance. Mastered utterly by Isabel's interpretation of him, Warburton becomes the generic Englishman who creates for them both a romantic scene:

> What she felt was that a territorial, a political, a social magnate had conceived the design of drawing her into the system in which he rather invidiously lived and moved. A certain instinct, not imperious, but persuasive, told her to resist . . . [She thought that it] would be very interesting to see something of his system from his own point of view; that on the other hand, however, there was . . . something stiff and stupid which would make it a burden. (Chap. 12)

Overestimating her own power of discrimination, Isabel presents the image of the superior aesthete, the unknown and unknowable woman, making the promise of totality seem available to Warburton while keeping it always just out of reach. Yet the text makes it clear that "her coldness was not the calculation of her effect – a game she played in a much smaller degree than would have seemed probable to many critics. It came from a certain fear" (Chap. 9). Isabel instinctively understands the social game, but her "coldness" – her overly intellectual approach to Warburton's desire – betrays a more desperate defense against (a fear of) her own emotions. Because desire calls up archaic fears of her own body (the seat of her earliest needs), she attributes an invidious rigidity to others when they express desire, and this allows her to evade similar traits in herself. As Ralph Touchett comments, Isabel adopts an acutely self-conscious strategy of detached appreciation in order not to feel. Her intellectual gift is double-edged. When men encourage her to be smart and independent, discovering in her a support for their own fantasies, they are only encouraging her to be more absent, disaffected, incapable of having an intimate relation with a man. Her incapacity forces Isabel to deny all knowledge of what Warburton desires of her: "'You're so good as to have a theory about me which I don't at all fill out . . . You're making fun of me'" (Chap. 9). In order to engage Warburton, she has to erase any knowledge of her body and desire. She seems to say, "I don't fill out; there is no vast (vaginal) design in me."

Even Ralph, sexually impotent and intellectually ignored, finds a way to send tremors through Isabel's life. By giving her a legacy, he invites her to solidify what has been to this point the mere illusion of power. Money makes Isabel's claim to mastery real, but such reality allows her only the most qualified pleasure: "'Yes, I'm afraid . . . A large fortune means freedom, and I'm afraid of that. . . . I'm not sure it's not a greater happiness to be powerless'" (Chap. 21). No sooner does she receive the gift than her faith in her freedom wavers.[17] Ralph's call to action might be thought of as a symbolically sexual demand, one that asks that she reveal the full power of her intelligence. But the idea of her "general" remarkableness – a more private, fantastic gratification of self-esteem – cannot withstand such an unwelcome collision with reality. Unable to channel vague desires into active social achievements and relations, Isabel is ready to sign over responsibility for her primitive desires, as well as her money, to Gilbert Osmond's account.

This too suggests that independence is a narcissistic construct — anxious, evasive, and linked to irresolvable dependency.

James shows us what no one character in the novel ever fully appreciates: that Isabel is diminished, not enhanced, by the fact that intimations of sexuality are impossible for her. Her ego hides an inner emptiness. Isabel is saying, "I cannot trust my first youth, for the maternal root of love is abandonment and annulment; therefore, I will protect myself with the loving care that I give to myself." She believes more deeply than she knows that "One should try to be one's own best friend and to give one's self, in this manner, distinguished company" (Chap. 6). Though this is a fine sentiment, Isabel is committed, without real freedom of choice, to an inhibition which passes in her own mind for self-reliance. Her psychological reality, though subtle and frequently disguised, plays itself out with the inevitability of tragedy.

The Return of the Phallic Mother

In the sheltering stability of the marital home, Isabel has the opportunity not only to become a mother but also to have a "mother" in her husband. In the psychoanalytic view, it is quite usual for women to marry parental substitutes, both mother and father. What is more unusual is for the "maternal" husband to become, due to his character and the woman's archaic conflicts, the bad mother all over again, thus upsetting many of the positive psychological ideals associated with marriage. But it is Osmond and Madame Merle, empowered by Isabel with the seductive and controlling traits of her own "bad" mother, who spring the marriage trap, exploit Isabel's vulnerabilities, and guarantee the circumstances of her unhappy future.

The absent mother, by being unavailable, wields great power in both the gratifying and frustrating fantasies of a child; but absence must eventually lead that child to other available sources of maternal power, whether good or bad. In either case, the transfer is complex; to heal through a substitute relation the damage incurred by the loss of reliable mothering is difficult, the more so when the wound is deeply buried and archaic need dominates, like a silent partner, all new relations with others, making them always and primarily substitute others.

It will be recalled that the transfer of all the attributes of the "good" mother to the father necessitates his idealization by the daughter. Chasseguet-Smirgel observes that, whatever compensations for the maternal deficit the girl might find in relation to the father, the idealization is programmed ultimately to fail because "[the father] does not yet have the attributes of the paternal role and plays only the role of a substitute for the mother."[18] In other words, the father may substitute for the good mother, but he is also heir to the emotional ambivalence that has not been resolved in relation to the bad mother.

I would argue that Merle initiates Isabel's return to archaic origins by enacting the role of the envied and feared maternal object that propels her towards her ambiguous husband, who is both idealized father and bad mother. Osmond absorbs Isabel's maternal ambivalence: he not only performs for her the role of the good mother by becoming the overvalued (superior) object of her love; but also, as a paternal figure, he inherits the tensions that Isabel has been unable to resolve toward the absent phallic mother. Their marital relations become sadomasochistic to the degree that Isabel confuses her obedience to Osmond's patriarchal law (the superego) with submission to the punishing maternal imago. Also, Isabel's submission to Osmond leads to narcissistic rivalry with him, and to their mutual objectification. Her relation to her husband is neurotic: a search *for* and flight *from* that repeats (within the context of adult sexual and social relations) the earliest relation to the envied and feared mother.

Madame Merle begins to cast her design on Isabel as the spell of a more perfect and gratifying self-possession − more narcissistic than Isabel herself, and at first worthy of imitation:

> Before luncheon, always, Madame Merle was engaged; Isabel admired and envied her rigid possession of her morning. Our heroine had always passed for a person of resources and had taken a certain pride in being one; but she wandered, as by the wrong side of the wall of a private garden, round the enclosed talents, accomplishments, aptitudes of Madame Merle. She found herself desiring to

145

emulate them, and in twenty such ways this lady presented herself as a model. (Chap. 19)

Though seeming to express Madame Merle's perfect self-sufficiency, on examination the passage gives us something quite different. There is, for example, the somewhat awkward phrase, "her rigid possession of her morning." Madame Merle would seem to possess an interval, not subjectivity; in this and other ways the text indicates how her life is lived entirely at the surface. For Madame Merle, an essential self – the sequestered domain of interiority – is a fiction. There is privacy and secrecy, but nothing private. She represents her talents on the outside. Since Madame Merle makes a performance out of her talent for privacy, Isabel imagines that there must also be a powerful self within the garden that is worth guarding (a reflection of her own wishful fantasies, never tested, of hidden plenitude within). Isabel might become even more proficient at her own self-protective and isolating superiority by imitating Merle. But Madame Merle's inviolate formal structure inspires in Isabel not only an oddly grandiose fantasy of personal largesse, but also a sense of envious wandering, of orbiting without ever finding what she needs in order to assume her authentic subjectivity.

This image of an invested exclusion is buttressed by the fantasy of rarity. Isabel's walking round an image of completion is also an admission of lack, is in fact a precise representation of her own inner emptiness and absolute need for the thing she has never had: a tenderly maternal atmosphere. She is always on the other side of the wall, consigned to the outer surface of what she most desires. In Isabel's relation with Madame Merle, absence inspires need, and need propels desire. Madame Merle becomes an idealized substitute object, and (more importantly) the idea of a structuring maternal presence – something that would begin to transform egoic armor into subjectivity. The terrible irony is that Madame Merle is a rigid structure, not a maternal subject whom Isabel can love and be loved by. To paraphrase Wallace Stevens, Isabel idealizes the nothingness that is present (Madame Merle as rigid and empty), compelled to do so by the nothingness that is not (the maternal subject). "If Isabel was sometimes moved to gape at her friend aspiringly and despairingly it was not so much because she desired herself to shine as because she wished to hold up the lamp for Madame Merle" (Chap. 19). Her need to be a lamp-bearer for Madame Merle suggests Isabel's willingness to submit to cold structure as a means of repairing maternal absence.

The obverse of Isabel's idealization of Madame Merle is frustration – disappointment felt towards the private and privative maternal substitute – that repeats the earliest failure of maternal gratification (the source of narcissistic injury). Isabel's frustrated need makes its inevitable appearance during her trip with Madame Merle to Greece and Egypt. Narration of the tour is introduced by Isabel's apology to Mrs. Touchett for not stopping in Florence, to which Mrs. Touchett responds with the following sentiment: "One either did the thing or one didn't, and what one 'would' have done belonged to the sphere of the irrelevant, like the idea of a future life or of the origin of things" (Chap. 31). Aunt Lydia's seemingly perfunctory response actually betrays the tour's dominant theme: origins.

Special attention is given to Madame Merle's sexual career, its beginnings and decline. "The late M. Merle, a positive adventurer . . . though originally so plausible . . . had taken advantage, years before, of her youth"; and consequently, Merle's morality had "been acquired at the court of some kingdom in decadence" (Chap. 31). This emphasis on the East, on "the origin of things," on freshness as opposed to "decadence," on the "original plausibility" of sexuality, again directs the reader to Isabel's parents – first to Mr. Archer, also a "positive adventurer" who, taking advantage of Isabel's youth, failed to provide a solid basis for development in a dependable paternal relation; and again to Mrs. Archer, since Madame Merle notices that in the most serene locations "Isabel traveled rapidly and recklessly; she was like a thirsty person draining cup after cup" (Chap. 31). Isabel's hunger for scenes is rendered as a primal, oral need, especially since what Isabel *drinks* are places, locations, in fact "the most classic sites." The maternal body is just such a "classic site," the first in time; that Isabel lost psychological contact with the nourishment received

147

there certainly helps to generate the intellectual "incoherence [that] prevailed in her" (Chap. 31). "Incoherence" in this context symptomatically expresses how insatiable desire can make Isabel appear out of control, compulsively miming the urgency of her oral need in the presence of the surrogate mother. She is doomed, as Freud cautioned, to repeat what cannot or has not been revised.

Equally remarkable is the text's use of explicitly phallic terms to describe Madame Merle. Isabel wonders how

> a person so *éprouvée* could have kept so much of her freshness . . . She seemed to see it as professional, as slightly mechanical, carried about in its case like the fiddle of the virtuoso, or blanketed and bridled like the "favorite" of the jockey . . . There was a corner of the curtain that never was lifted; it was as if she had remained after all something of a public performer, condemned to emerge only in character and in costume. (Chap. 31)

Madame Merle does seem the master of her own performance of "freshness," and of her audience. Though Isabel ambivalently devalues Merle-as-mother and disdains her inferior sense of morality, she does so without emancipation from her. Isabel's tragedy is that she can accurately estimate neither Merle's real intentions nor her own childish constructions (in relation to the pre-Oedipal phallic mother): Isabel's infinite susceptibility to Merle is her susceptibility to her own archaic fantasies. Lacan has given us the psychoanalytic truism that the phallus can play its role only when veiled. Madame Merle, as a version of the pre-Oedipal mother who entices by holding out on the promise of desire gratified, is made more powerful by concealing that she does not have "it" (the phallus). This structuring principle is crucial: it serves to determine gender relations under patriarchy, and allows for the fantasy of wholeness by concealing the fact that desire can never be entirely realized. Madame Merle is veiled, for only then can she command Isabel; as we are told, "there was a corner of the curtain that never was lifted."

But the passage can be read for psychological meanings even more primitive. Madame Merle's performing the role of phallic mother relies heavily on Isabel's oral neediness. Isabel's astonishment that Madame Merle can be both fresh and *éprouvée* is actually a deeper complaint against the ambiguous feminine (the mother who has and withholds), something that becomes apparent by placing freshness and *éprouvée* together, or by reading their verbal relation as a condensation which raises the possibility of a deeper connection between contradictory ideas. The notion of a freshness *éprouvée* (freshness ruined, injured, aggrieved, lost) is curious but telling. As a description of Madame Merle, it suggests her association with an inaugural loss, a ruined source, but the condensation is lifted from Isabel's unconscious text. A semblance of freshness, a promise of something life-giving, persists in Madame Merle. Yet she is the absence which disappoints, thus inviting the child's repudiation; she is the lack which paradoxically inflames desire for what cannot be and manufactures hope in improbable and frustrating relations.

Osmond may direct Merle as his resourceful virtuoso, but as the pre-Oedipal reading makes clear, the primitive mother has composed the score. Isabel's attraction to Osmond is thus mediated through Madame Merle. Though Osmond is even less nourishing than she, Isabel loves Osmond both for *what* he withholds and *because* he withholds. He becomes the more severe and compelling version of her want: "Madame Merle had had that note of rarity, but what quite other power it immediately gained when sounded by a man! It was not so much what he said and did, but rather what he *withheld* . . . he was *an original* without being an eccentric" (Chap. 24, my emphasis).

Isabel adores Osmond's "originality": he is unique among men, but also uniquely ambiguous in her eyes. He is on the one hand rather compulsive and sadistic; he would revenge his envy on others, manipulate them to his own ends, and fit them like functionaries to his private system of desire. He is on the other hand highly attentive to Isabel, even mild in his solicitude. "'Go everywhere,' he said at last, in a low, kind voice; 'do everything; get everything out of life. Be happy – be triumphant'" (Chap. 29). As both admiring parent and hard disciplinarian, Osmond's originality consists in his *not being an original*, but in being rather the perfect vessel for Isabel's maternal fantasies, fantasies that include the image of superior power and the hope of participating in maternal omnipotence without being destroyed by it. Osmond suits Isabel in other ways, and James's portrait of their psychological partnership grows increasingly subtle. Osmond can be idealized for his weakness, "for his very poverties dressed out as honors" (Chap. 34); Isabel again transforms paternal frailties into strengths. He is both superior and weak, ungratifying yet promising through a controlling vigilance to elude the maternal threat; Isabel could have no other husband than the maternal Osmond.

It is Osmond's "sickness" that draws Isabel to him, just as she is drawn to maternal power-in-deprivation. "He had consulted his taste in everything – his taste alone perhaps, as a sick man consciously incurable consults at last only his lawyer: that was what made him so different from everyone else. . . . He was critical of himself as well as of others, and, exact[ed] a good deal of others, to think them agreeable" (Chap. 24). Though idealized as superior, Osmond is critical, unavailable, uninterested, and self-centered: the feminized patriarch possesses many of the distinctive traits of the omnipotent phallic mother. Isabel can be sure that Osmond *will take care* of her feelings. Indeed, he binds them in a strict corset of taste. In the following reflection, Isabel intimates some of the deeper reasons she has to please Osmond during their courtship:

> A part of Isabel's fatigue came from the effort to appear as intelligent as she believed Madame Merle had described her, and from the fear (very unusual with her) of exposing – not her ignorance . . . but her possible grossness of perception. It would have annoyed her to express a liking for something he, in his superior enlightenment, would think she oughtn't to like; or to pass by something at which the truly initiated mind would arrest itself. She had no wish to fall into that grotesqueness – in which she had seen women (and it was a warning) serenely, yet ignobly, flounder. (Chap. 24)

Her anxious submission to a superior partner allows her to benefit in two ways. First, she participates in Osmond's grandeur by taking him as her narcissistic object: she believes herself chosen by Madame Merle because of her superiority, and will strive to resemble Osmond in *his* fineness. Also, he rescues her from the more dangerous fate of uncontrolled feeling. The first step of this more precipitous fall would begin with the descent into grotesqueness –

in which women, without ever knowing, lovelessly flounder. Isabel lets Osmond assume the function of her punishing conscience; now he will restrain her *other* self, that deeply felt wrongness of unruly desire and unconscious hatred associated with being female.

But it is also in hope of having *what is not* that Isabel allows herself, through her husband, dreams of being received by and *becoming* herself a good mother.

> There had been an indefinable beauty about him – in his situation, in his mind, in his face. She had felt at the same time that he was helpless and ineffectual, but the feeling had taken the form of a tenderness which was the very flower of respect. He was like a skeptical voyager strolling on the beach while he waited for the tide, looking seaward yet not putting to sea. . . . She would launch his boat for him; she would be his providence . . . As she looked back at the passion of those full weeks she perceived in it a kind of maternal strain – the happiness of a woman who felt that she was a contributor, that she came with charged hands. (Chap. 42)

Osmond exists here as an uncertain figure empty of positive qualities, a querulous space that seems to invite Isabel to invent him out of her desire. His indefiniteness becomes his charm, the vessel that might bear them both to a saving maternity. Ineffectual, Osmond can be idealized without fear.

The synthesis of ideality and frailty in a paternal figure (a father only by default) demonstrates how both vibrate to the maternal strain. The mother is the sea, of course, the encompassing element into which the "boat" (the husband) is launched. This ubiquitous feminine substance of pleasure and passion will envelop Osmond and develop him to infinity. Through Isabel's charged hands, which enhance Osmond's "indefinable beauty" (his dazzling originality), he is permitted to embark upon the joyful pleasure of the maternal absolute. Holding the key to Osmond's happiness, as she believes, Isabel regresses toward a very private vision of paradise. Through her husband she is once again related to her own phantasmal mother, and there is no greater pleasure, Isabel imagines, than to be received again by the good mother.

Absolute devotion to Osmond leads to its opposite: the acquisi-

151

tion of Osmond by Isabel as property. "The finest – in the sense of being the subtlest – manly organism she had ever known had become her property, and the recognition of her having but to put out her hands and take it had been originally a sort of act of devotion" (Chap. 42). The fantasy of omnipotence regained exacts the masochistic price of serving Osmond. Paradoxically, Osmond is both reified and distinguished, almost exalted, for his fineness: Isabel approaches Osmond as if supplicating to a fetish. The double act of reifying and placing him above her has both self-aggrandizing and self-punishing psychological implications.

The fantasy of husband as idealized property suggests that Isabel has difficulty conceiving of herself and Osmond as adult sexual beings in reciprocal and yet independent relation to one another. Either she feels herself to be an extension of him, or she takes him as her property. Both tendencies indicate Isabel's lack of a stable, independent female identity. As we have seen, the result of an unintegrated femininity (identification with the phallic mother) is the contamination of adult sexuality by the early narcissistic relation to the body – the persistence of the influences of the un-differentiated, pregenital state. This, Irene Fast suggests, leads the woman to two related narcissistic fantasies: "That the man is all and she is nothing," and that "[she is] narcissistically complete and the man is utterly lacking."[19] The fantasy of the launch allows Isabel to see herself as all, Osmond as nothing; however, earlier she had given herself the opposite: "she had made herself small, pretending there was less of her than there really was" (Chap. 42). In her conscious construction, Isabel seems to manage everything: she bestows power on Osmond and makes herself small before what she has made powerful. Osmond merely obliges by fitting her to her narrow place in his world. But it is only through him and in submission to him that she can hope to attain her greater self.

Isabel's devotion to Osmond, her idolatry, demonstrates that she has abandoned actualization of her own aspirations, and settled instead for the fixed symbolism of the fetish. That is, she invests a substitute object with her own self-realizing power. But why? Maria Torok explains: "Coveting a thing is precisely the same thing as demonstrating to the imago [in Isabel's case, Osmond as image of the phallic mother] the renunciation of an act."[20] In order to avoid an open show of aggression and risk retaliation, Isabel submits to the authority of Osmond (as maternal image) and sacrifices self-realization by insisting on the exorbitant value of Osmond-as-thing. She renounces not only her *femininity* but also her female *identity* — unconsciously regarded as an act of aggression — and protects her continued dependence on the subjectivity of a greater other. The untenable circularity of this position is represented in its central contradiction, which appears to be almost an article of faith — namely, that Isabel can devalue and control only by overvaluing and submitting. Her illusion of mastery is fragile indeed, requiring as it does perpetual evasion of this contradiction. Her incentive is compelling, however. In hope of obscuring her dependency on a pre-Oedipal maternal body, Isabel objectifies Osmond by permitting her own objectification, and tries to empower herself by surrendering all power to him. She can neither consciously admit her desire nor forthrightly challenge her subjugation, but can only attempt to circumvent the maternal influence and perhaps magically confound its direct (and psychologically deadly) affront to her already vulnerable sense of self.

For Isabel, love must entail grandiosity and self-punishment, and her unconscious need to submit and (by submission) keep alive hopes for eventual pleasure is profoundly masochistic. Masochism is not, as is most commonly thought, the love of pain, but rather the unconscious conviction that the pleasure one seeks must be punished, and that submission to retribution, by coming first, must inevitably lead to its opposite, the unconscious desired satisfaction.[21] Masochistic submission also liberates Isabel to cultivate her unconscious, unrealized fantasies (to be dependent without risking the annihilation which passivity entails), but only by confining her. She neutralizes the absent mother's power by becoming other herself — a thing appended to the mother's power, a phallus.

In order to exist unthreatened Isabel submits; but by submitting, by becoming Osmond's phallus, she becomes an empty function in another's (the husband's, the mother's) system of desire. We are told that in responding to Osmond's domination Isabel "had resisted of course; . . . she had pleaded the cause . . . of other instincts and longings, of quite another ideal," seeming almost to beg for real sustenance as opposed to symbolism (Chap. 42). In the end, her submission, though clouded with resentment, is beyond question: "Her mind was to be his — attached to his own like a small garden-plot to a deer-park" (Chap. 42).

Isabel's relation to Osmond is upheld in the beginning by a replacement of sexual passion with intimations of ascetic transport. This is evoked in the scene of Isabel's supplication within the grandly ornamented enclosure of St. Peter's Basilica. The dome's sublimity, the air thickened with incense, the light reflecting from marble and gilt, at once solicits and resists comprehension ("her conception of greatness rose and dizzily rose"); the reader is unprepared for the remarkable ease with which Isabel approaches the sublime. In the security of St. Peter's it is all right, or so Isabel believes, to "feel like an atom." Osmond's reaction is telling: "'I suppose it's the right way to feel everywhere, when one *is* nobody. But I like it in a church as little as anywhere else'" (Chap. 27). Wholly dependent on his own will to collect and appreciate the world in its pieces, according to his design, Osmond detests feeling overwhelmed, that sense of being nobody in another's greater design. But Isabel, as nun or nobody, is content to all but vanish into the vast powerful sea of St. Peter's. What could be more asexual, regressive, and submissive than this oceanic atomization? According to psychoanalysis, to *be* is to be *sexual*. Isabel would relinquish the demands of identity (which is necessarily sexual after adolescence); she would be cared for without having to be anybody. St. Peter's dome brings Isabel, the child, unto it: "she gazed and wondered like a child or a peasant" (Chap. 27). It satisfies symbolically her archaic passive desires, as her marriage might have done, had the malevolent maternal image not been so necessary a part of the contract.

Osmond has seen firsthand Isabel's desire to be lost, atomlike, in a larger structure. By assuming the role of that greater structure and disciplining Isabel's desires, he fits her need into his own design. He also exploits Isabel's narcissistically inspired devotion by becoming the one who solicits her "tenderness for things that were passive and weak." This is the impulse she idealizes in Osmond and identifies with in Pansy. Not only does she want to be Pansy's mother, but also, in the depths of her nature, "in a very out-of-the-way place," she is much like Pansy: a tender submissive thing (Chap. 4). Pansy does not know that she (Pansy) is a woman, only that she is her father's woman; as she says, "'Am I not meant for you, papa?'" (Chap. 22). Isabel is meant for him as well, despite her anger, but only after her phallic attachment to the primal mother is properly transferred. Thus Isabel's "unquenchable desire to please" locates a central form of self-alienation: Isabel as the helpless and ineffectual appendage of the phantasmal mother, projected into the world of the fiction as the cold, ungratifying, and controlling Osmond.

Interlocking neurotic distortions are thus at work in the novel: Isabel's masochistic submission, and Osmond's sadistic appropriation of her passive desire. In this context it is impossible to speak of Isabel's having assumed responsibility for her subjectivity. It has been surrendered in her relations with Madame Merle and Osmond, who seem to provide hope of compensation: satisfaction both of her desire to please (to be another's desire), and of her desire to think well of herself (to recover the indefinable beauty of a wholeness beyond subjectivity). Merle and Osmond are Isabel's best readers, for they ignore her demand to be recognized for her singularity and listen instead to the inner meaning of her desire. What they offer is survival, perpetuation of an unresolvable dilemma, nothing more. On the other hand, in effecting their own ends and answering so perfectly to Isabel's need, they little suspect that her need is itself so insidiously reductive, objectifying them even as they exploit it. The sadomasochistic circle, for as long as it works, obscures the mother within.

Isabel's Narrative: A Vessel for Absence

The Portrait does not resolve the question of maternal absence; but by prompting the reader to ask the question, it demonstrates the perfectly untenable position of the mother *en systeme:* the mother is a female subject unable to meet either her own or her daughter's personal needs. The mother was a formidable presence in the Victorian family, but a presence with little legitimate power. Her marginalization, devaluation, and virtual exclusion from the patriarchal sphere of intellectual and social authority only assured her role as the enigmatic object of wish, fear, and fantasy. True to the novel's tragic vision, the text, with a keen and subtle eye, fixes Isabel's psychological fate.

Two passages toward the end of the novel are of special interest. The first describes Isabel's unmasking of Merle at Mother Catherine's convent; the second presents Isabel's reflections on the beginning of her European life at Gardencourt. In these passages James captures the dynamic of Isabel Archer's psychological life according to the three themes developed here: maternal absence, masochism, and narcissism. One can also see why there is so little social "justice" in Isabel's choice to remain in her marriage, why the justice in her "freedom" of choice is really a mystification of the psychology of female submission under patriarchy. James knew that women, given such limited options, would rationalize their bad marriages and empty dreams in order to endure; but he also understood that the alternative to female submission cannot be a simple exercise of mastery by the ego. Isabel Archer, like a musician with a sorely limited repertoire, is left to repeat both of these self-imprisoning gestures, because fear of the unloving other, of maternal husband and absent mother, has so thoroughly restricted the boundaries of improvisation.

According to Carren Kaston, Isabel does not really know how she feels about Osmond, and there may be no good reason for remaining with him. Confronted by Henrietta's assertion that both her suffering and her misplaced nobility may in fact be supererogatory, Isabel responds, " 'In default of a better [reason], my having promised will do' " (Chap. 52). Lacking legitimate motives, she must justify her lack of freedom: self-denial can be pursued, but only out of an upright belief in the preciousness it confers. At the convent it becomes clear that her failure in relation to Merle fixes Isabel in this belief and ensures her return to Osmond.

Through an interplay of reflection and absence, parodic of the mirroring of mother and child in pre-Oedipal life, Isabel *sees* Merle *seeing* her, and by seeing and being seen each is diminished: "Isabel saw it all distinctly as if it had been reflected in a large clear glass. . . . Madame Merle had lost her pluck and saw before her the *phantom of exposure*" (Chap. 52, my emphasis). In the glass, Isabel and Merle double one another – specular partners, but also mere reflections. Though Isabel's thought and vision are addressed to Merle, they rebound by exposing Merle as less; Isabel becomes herself a phantom, a harbinger of the emptiness she glimpses in Merle, both an agent and a victim of what is for the moment their shared insubstantiality. The self-reflexive exchange acquires a "taste of dishonor," becomes a silent "confession of helplessness." Both Merle and Isabel have been made functionaries of patriarchy. But Merle's mediation, which exploited the power given her as mother, recapitulates maternal abandonment with deadening clarity. Isabel sees, then must look away: "She saw, in the crude light . . . that she had been an applied handled hung-up tool, as senseless and convenient as mere shaped wood and iron. . . . If she had turned and spoken, she would have said something that would hiss like a lash. But she closed her eyes, and then *the hideous vision dropped*" (Chap. 52, my emphasis). Whether confronted here with the hideous vision of Merle's helpless cruelty or by the prospect of her own, Isabel is herself helpless to retaliate: silently, with eyes closed, she confesses the ineffability of her rage. Lost, dishonored, powerless souls, Madame Merle and Isabel establish between them a strange, alienating misalliance: their dissociation serves only to expose a deeper involution, an incongruous congruity of identity. Merle, exposed as an adulteress, must be exiled to America to ensure that Isabel's return to monogamous domesticity can itself be rationalized. However, Merle's banishment does not mark Isabel's freedom from what Merle represented. On the contrary, it dramatizes Isabel's reinternalization of the projected image of the bad mother – returned to Isabel, its sender, in the form of malign emptiness.

The unresolved identification leads Isabel to a crisis of self-annihilation: death as an archaic fantasy of escape, the brute result of aggression's unthinkable release. "To cease utterly, to give it all up and not know anything more − this idea was as sweet as the vision of a cool bath in a marble tank, in a darkened chamber, in a hot land" (Chap. 53). Here, death is a regression − a dream of unqualified access to the maternal body, itself a cool dark place insulated from the desert of human relations, where the demands of personality begin. However, Isabel cannot name and disempower the destructiveness of maternal lack, and thus emancipate herself. "Her intelligence dropped, from literal inability to say what it was that Madame Merle had been. . . . It concerned Isabel no more" (Chap. 53). Suppressing rather than facing her hatred of Merle, Isabel literally loses her remarkable strength of "vision" and "intelligence" − both are "dropped." Active self-inhibition is perceived as innocent passivity, and her faculties fall away as if of themselves. In her desire to be helpless but cared for, Isabel submits herself to dissociated self-pacification.

> It might be desirable to get quite away, really away, further away than little grey-green England, but this privilege was evidently to be denied her. Deep in her soul − deeper than any appetite for renunciation − was the sense that life would be her business for a long time to come. And at moments there was something inspiring, almost enlivening, in the conviction. It was a proof of strength − it was a proof she should some day be happy again. (Chap. 53)

Though this passage seems at first to suggest an innocent desire to go somewhere, anywhere, it quickly becomes clear that the impulse for unplanned holidays has been replaced by depressive fantasy. The clear opposition between "renunciation" and the business of "life" makes it apparent that to renounce can only be morbid, that to get "really away" is an act of self-dispossession. In retaining the irresolvable identification with the mother, Isabel holds onto the fantasied "privilege" of death (utter passivity), yet assumes limited control over "her appetite for renunciation" by yielding submissively to life. Since one cannot get away without dying, this business of life must be endured, at least until endurance itself becomes enlivening − proof that the power of endurance ought to bestow happiness on the sufferer. Isabel's passivity follows from having to swallow unexpressed anger; and in this depressed state, she sees the plain fact of her suffering as proof that she should someday be happy.

This train of thought might best be understood as a form of masochistic reasoning — pain, by coming first, entitles one to happiness. Isabel's masochism propels her toward a "mutilated glimpse of her future":

> To live only to suffer — only to feel the injury of life *repeated and enlarged* — it seemed to her she was too valuable, too capable, for that. Then she wondered if it were vain and stupid to think so well of herself. When had it ever been a guarantee to be valuable? Wasn't all history full of the destruction of precious things? Wasn't it much more probable that if one were fine one would suffer? It involved then perhaps an admission that one had a certain grossness; *but* Isabel recognized, as it passed before her eyes, the quick vague shadow of a long future. She *should* never escape; she *should* last to the end. (Chap. 54, my emphasis)

Is this glimpse of the future "mutilated" because Isabel cannot foresee what will happen to her, or because her own vision (which must be dropped for fear of violence) is the glimpse that mutilates? Repeating and enlarging the (narcissistic) injury has mutilated Isabel's past and present and predisposes her view of the future toward the interlocking neurotic distortions of masochism and narcissism.

The passage demonstrates how wasted fineness, once conceived of as profoundly possible, may initiate profound possibility — how suffering becomes a basis for hope. The illogical movement of the passage, its redemptive method, is disguised by a few skillful equivocations. Isabel seems to confront certain realities of history: the destruction of precious things (her own vulnerability) and the shared "grossness" of human sufferers, herself among them. What happens is quite different, however. Her initial question concerns "guarantees," as if to say none exist; the second admits of destruction of precious things; the third, however, initiates an ingenious response to and inversion of both, while seeming to support an admirable realism. The shift is subtle: destruction (of precious things) becomes a probability of suffering and proof of fineness; an arbitrary death is equated with, and replaced by, the very different idea of "fineness" suffering. The result, the negation of death by suffering, makes possible the pivotal phrase "but Isabel recognized," and the shift toward an inevitable future extending vaguely toward an end which cannot be death, an end which is not an end at all. In a few short lines realistic assessment has become an (apparently logical) assurance of necessary immortality. The sequence, taken as a whole, is a tour de force of oneiric "logic," designed to evade a lack of freedom: fineness leads to suffering; suffering is common, admitting of a certain grossness, not fineness at all; but suffering can redeem grossness and make it fine again — not only can, but should. Destruction has been negated by suffering; therefore, as long as one suffers one has a future, and the "end" is deferred, presumably forever. She will last and last, proving and improving her fineness, becoming, almost like the lovers on Keats's urn, happy and happier still. Isabel is indeed a precious *thing,* and never so narcissistic as when resolidifying her egoic armor.

What Isabel has never escaped is the importance of maternal absence. She cannot hope to love herself as her mother should have done except by entering into a hopeless cycle of psychological stagnation — of asceticism promising objectified grandeur. It is not within her power to undo patriarchy's devaluation of the mother, or her own motherless past. In concert with her maternal husband, she will perform in perpetuity the circular rituals of ownership and objectification, freedom and imprisonment, aggression and submission. In Osmond, the maternal body becomes the site of Isabel's suffering, her cross and her only hope.

NOTES

1. Leon Edel, *Henry James: A Life* (New York: Harper and Row, 1985), p. 259.
2. John Carlos Rowe, *The Theoretical Dimensions of Henry James* (Madison: University of Wisconsin Press, 1984), pp. 32–3.
3. Jean Strouse, *Alice James: A Biography* (Boston: Houghton Mifflin, 1980), p. 27.

4. Jacques Lacan, "Aggressivity in Psychoanalysis," *Ecrits – A Selection*, as quoted in M. Guy Thompson, *The Death of Desire: A Study of Psychopathology* (New York: New York University Press, 1985), p. 19.

5. Narcissism is one of the most controversial concepts in psychoanalysis. My discussion of the idea of narcissism relies largely on Lacan's theory, rather than on that of the American ego psychologist and object relations theorist Otto Kernberg. Kernberg views the ego as an organ with both optimal developmental potential and nonconflictual adaptational capabilities; also, he regards strong ego integration as a major criterion of psychological health, and contrasts this with immaturities of ego structure in narcissistic personality disorder. While American psychoanalysts tend not to theorize desire or the subject, Lacan believes that the ego actually obscures subjectivity (which cannot be equated with the concept of self), and he stresses that the ego, far from being an organ of adaptation, is part of the id, and the object of unconscious desires, narcissistic illusions, and defensive conflict. In contrast, Kernberg describes narcissistic personality organization as an extreme form of "ego weakness," typified by particularly primitive defense mechanisms, unstable boundaries, and pathological fusing of "ideal" and "actual" self-images (Kernberg, *Borderline Conditions and Pathological Narcissism* [New York: Aronson, 1985], pp. 227–354). Though Lacan is categorical (the ego is always a narcissistic object), Kernberg's description of narcissism is in many ways more severe. Ironically, this results in part from the theoretical requirement to distinguish the healthy from the pathological ego. What is in fact open to question is Kernberg's initial assumption – the idea of the ego as a strong, adaptive structure. (See Thompson's discussion, "The Idolatry of the Ego," in *The Death of Desire*.)

6. Erik Erikson, as quoted in Nancy Chodorow, *The Reproduction of Mothering* (Berkeley: University of California Press, 1978), p. 229.

7. Janine Chasseguet-Smirgel, "Freud and Female Sexuality," *International Journal of Psychoanalysis* 57 (1976): 285.

8. Helene Deutsch, *Selected Problems of Adolescence* (New York: International Universities Press, 1978), p. 117.

9. M. Guy Thompson, *The Death of Desire*, p. 75.

10. Sigmund Freud as quoted in Janine Chasseguet-Smirgel, "Feminine Guilt and the Oedipus Complex," *Female Sexuality: New Psychoanalytic Views* (London: Virago Press, 1981), p. 98.

11. Ibid., pp. 98–9.

12. Moses Laufer and M. Eglé Laufer, *Adolescence and Developmental Breakdown: A Psychoanalytic View* (New Haven: Yale University Press, 1984), p. 111.
13. Janine Chasseguet-Smirgel, "Feminine Guilt and the Oedipus Complex," p. 119.
14. Moses and M. Eglé Laufer, *Adolescence and Developmental Breakdown*, p. 62.
15. Luce Irigaray, *Speculum of the Other Woman*, trans. Gillian C. Gill (Ithaca: Cornell University Press, 1985), p. 78.
16. Sigmund Freud, "The Most Prevalent Form of Degradation in Erotic Life," *Creativity and the Unconscious* (New York: Harper and Row, 1958).
17. I am indebted to Carren Kaston for this observation in her feminist discussion of *The Portrait* in *Imagination and Desire in the Novels of Henry James* (New Brunswick: Rutgers University Press, 1984), p. 44.
18. Janine Chasseguet-Smirgel, "Feminine Guilt and the Oedipus Complex," p. 119.
19. Irene Fast, "Gender Differentiation in Girls," *International Journal of Psychoanalysis* 60 (1979): 451.
20. Maria Torok, "The Significance of Penis Envy in Women," *Female Sexuality: New Psychoanalytic Views*, p. 141.
21. Theodor Reik, *Masochism in Modern Man* (New York: Grove Press, 1957).

Notes on Contributors

Beth Sharon Ash is an Assistant Professor of English at the University of Chicago. She has published articles on modern critical theory and is currently working on a psychosocial reading of Joseph Conrad's life and major novels.

Alfred Habegger, Professor of English at the University of Kansas at Lawrence, is the author of *Gender, Fantasy, and Realism in American Literature* (1982) and *Henry James and the "Woman Business"* (1989). He is currently working on a biography of Henry James, Sr.

Donatella Izzo, who teaches English and American literature at the Università Degli Studi "Gabriele D'Annunzio" in Pescara, Italy, is the author of *Henry James* (1981). Cristina Bacchilega is an Assistant Professor of English at the University of Hawaii at Manoa.

Joel Porte, formerly chairman of the English Department at Harvard University, where he taught for many years, is currently Ernest I. White Professor of American Studies and Humane Letters at Cornell University. He is the author of *The Romance in America* (1969), *Representative Man: Ralph Waldo Emerson in His Time* (1979), and *In Respect to Egotism: Studies in American Romantic Writing,* forthcoming in 1990 from Cambridge University Press.

William Veeder is Professor of English at the University of Chicago. He has written and edited books on James, Mary Shelley, Victorian feminism, and Robert Louis Stevenson. He is currently at work on a study of Anglo-American Gothic fiction, 1885–1914.

Selected Bibliography

Readers interested in threading their way through the voluminous critical response to *The Portrait of a Lady* are fortunate in having at their disposal a number of collections of essays on the novel that also include useful bibliographical information. Among these are: William T. Stafford, ed., *Perspectives on James's The Portrait of a Lady* (New York: New York University Press, 1967); Peter Buitenhuis, ed., *Twentieth Century Interpretations of The Portrait of a Lady* (Englewood Cliffs, N.J.: Prentice-Hall, 1968); Lyall H. Powers, ed., *Merrill Studies in The Portrait of a Lady* (Columbus, Ohio: Merrill, 1970); Robert D. Bamberg, ed., *The Portrait of a Lady,* Norton Critical Edition (New York: Norton, 1975); Alan Shelston, ed., *Washington Square and The Portrait of a Lady: A Casebook* (London: Macmillan, 1984); Daniel Mark Fogel, ed., *The Henry James Review* 7 (1986): 1–195 (this last contains a comprehensive annotated bibliography compiled by Marion Richmond); and *Henry James's The Portrait of a Lady,* ed. Harold Bloom (New York: Chelsea House, 1987).

The following is a representative list of studies of the novel that, in the opinion of the editor, provide a good introduction to the secondary literature. Further suggestions can be culled from the notes to the essays in this volume.

Allen, Elizabeth. *A Woman's Place in the Novels of Henry James.* New York: St. Martin's Press, 1984.

Auchard, John. *Silence in Henry James: The Heritage of Symbolism and Decadence.* University Park, Pa.: Pennsylvania State University Press, 1986.

Chase, Richard. "The Lesson of the Master," in *The American Novel and Its Tradition.* New York: Doubleday, 1957. Reprinted in Stafford, *Perspectives.*

Edel, Leon. Introduction to *The Portrait of a Lady.* Boston: Houghton Mifflin, 1956.

Esch, Deborah. "'Understanding Allegories': Reading *The Portrait of a Lady*," in *Henry James's The Portrait of a Lady*, pp. 131–53.

Galloway, David. *Henry James: The Portrait of a Lady*. London: Edward Arnold, 1967.

Gass, William H. "The High Brutality of Good Intentions." *Accent* 18 (1958): 62–71. Reprinted in Stafford, *Perspectives*, and Bamberg, Norton *Portrait*.

Habegger, Alfred. *Gender, Fantasy, and Realism in American Literature*. New York: Columbia University Press, 1982.

Long, Robert Emmet. *Henry James: The Early Novels*. Boston: Twayne Publishers, 1983.

Matthiessen, F. O. "The Painter's Sponge and the Varnish Bottle," in *Henry James: The Major Phase*. New York: Oxford University Press, 1944. Reprinted in Stafford, *Perspectives*, and Bamberg, Norton *Portrait*.

McMaster, Juliet. "The Portrait of Isabel Archer." *American Literature* 45 (1973): 50–66.

Niemtzow, Annette. "Marriage and the New Woman in *The Portrait of a Lady*." *American Literature* 47 (1975): 377–95.

Poirier, Richard. "*The Portrait of a Lady*," in Wallace Stegner, ed., *The American Novel from James Fenimore Cooper to William Faulkner*. New York: Basic Books, 1965.

Tanner, Tony. "The Fearful Self: Henry James's *The Portrait of a Lady*. *Critical Quarterly* 7 (1965): 205–19. Reprinted in Powers, *Studies*, and Shelston, *Casebook*.

Taylor, Gordon O. *The Passages of Thought: Psychological Representation in the American Novel, 1870–1900*. New York: Oxford University Press, 1969.

Van Ghent, Dorothy. *The English Novel: Form and Function*. New York: Holt, Rinehart, & Winston, 1953. Reprinted in Stafford, *Perspectives*, Powers, *Studies*, and Bamberg, Norton *Portrait*.

Weinstein, Philip M. *Henry James and the Requirements of the Imagination*. Cambridge, Mass.: Harvard University Press, 1971.

Weisbuch, Robert. *Atlantic Double-Cross*. Chicago: University of Chicago Press, 1986.